000115388

599.9
T

D0564449

DISCARD

High-Tech IDs

FROM FINGER SCANS TO VOICE PATTERNS

High-Tech IDs

FROM FINGER SCANS TO VOICE PATTERNS

By Salvatore Tocci

Franklin Watts
A Division of Grolier Publishing
New York ■ London ■ Hong Kong ■ Sydney
Danbury, Connecticut

Photographs ©: AP/Wide World Photos: 29 (Bob Child), 88 (Peter Cosgrove), 13 (David Longstreath), 35 (Lennox McLendon), 27 (Alan Mothner), 15 right (Orlin Wagner), 15 left, 74, 77 (Alexander Zemlianichenko); Courtesy of Ultra-Scan Corporation: 99; Grace Davies Photography: 9, 53, 56, 66, 71; Liaison Agency Inc.: 79 (George De Keerle), 49 (Eric Bazin), 38 (Spencer Grant), 12 (Hulton Getty), 25; Millenium Jet Inc.: 101; Photo Provided by Recognition Systems: 31, 43; Photo Researchers: 52 (Danny Brass/Science Source), cover (James King-Holmes/SPL), 64 (Hank Morgan/Science Source), 82 (Sinclair Stammers/SPL); Shanin Leeming: 110.

Illustrations by George Stewart: 18; Bob Italiano: 20; and Mike DiGiorgio: 47.

Visit Franklin Watts on the Internet at:
http://publishing.grolier.com

Library of Congress Cataloging-in-Publication Data

Tocci, Salvatore.
    High-tech IDs: from finger scans to voice patterns / by Salvatore Tocci.
        p. cm.
    Includes bibliographical references and index.
    Summary: Describes a variety of devices and systems used for identifying individuals, including finger and hand scans, iris and retinal scans, fingerprinting, DNA fingerprinting, and voice pattern recognition, and gives examples of how they are used.
    ISBN 0-531-11752-9 (lib. bdg.)   0-531-16462-4 (pbk)
    1. Biometry Juvenile literature. 2. Identification Juvenile literature. [1. Biometry.] I. Title.
QH323.5.T63   2000
599.9'4−dc21   99-37380
                                                                            CIP

©2000 Franklin Watts, a Division of Grolier Publishing.
All rights reserved. Published simultaneously in Canada.
Printed in the United States of America.
2 3 4 5 6 7 8 9 10 R 09 08 07 06 05 04 03 02 01 00

Contents

1 What Is Biometrics?

On August 17, 1994, the owners of a hotel discovered that $45,000 had been stolen from their money room the night before. Only fifteen hotel employees had authorized access to the locked room where the hotel kept cash receipts before depositing them in the bank. To enter the room, each person had to punch a personal identification number (PIN) into a keypad on the door and then swipe an access card through a reader, a device that reads information. How could an intruder possibly get into the room?

One of the employees with access to the money room was named Darren. He worked as an accountant at the hotel. Aware of how much cash was usually in the room, Darren often reminded his co-workers of the need for security. But Darren seemed to forget what he preached to the others.

Whenever he was in his own office, Darren hung his jacket on the back of the door. He kept his wallet in the pocket of the jacket. Inside his wallet were his money, his credit cards, and his access card to the money room.

The day before he left for a 2-week vacation, Darren entered the money room to take care of some business. Police believe that an intruder must have been watching Darren from a small closet across the hall. The intruder wrote down the numbers Darren punched into the keypad: 5-5-5-6-0-2-2. Later, when Darren briefly left his office, the intruder stole Darren's access card from the jacket hanging on the back of the door.

Armed with Darren's PIN and access card, the intruder could gain access to any room in the hotel—including the money room. The intruder must have known that Darren was about to go on vacation. Darren's departure fit in perfectly with the intruder's plan to steal cash from the money room.

Each time a person entered the money room, an entry was recorded in a log. The log showed that Darren entered the room on August 16, 1994, at 11:51 P.M. But Darren was actually away on vacation that night, hundreds of miles from the hotel.

The next day, an audit revealed that $45,000 was missing. Soon after Darren was told about the theft, he discovered that his access card was missing. The police never caught the intruder.

A New Type of Security System

After the robbery, the hotel re-evaluated its security system. The owners decided to install three hand scanners to control access to various locations in the hotel. The first reader allows access to employees who are authorized to enter the money room. The second reader permits a very small group of employees to enter both the money room and the vault inside where the money is stored. The third reader is located in the hotel's security office and is used to enroll new employees.

During the enrollment process, a hotel supervisor enters the employee's name and assigns a PIN. The supervisor determines the access areas, time periods, and reader locations that are available to each employee. The supervisor can also adjust the hand scanners to accommodate individual differences. For example, the settings can be adjusted to reduce the chances that an employee will be mistakenly rejected because a physical disability makes it difficult for the person to use the scanner.

To enroll, an employee places a hand on the scanner three separate times. The scanner creates a template, or record, of the features of that person's hand. The template is stored in a database. The employee must then test the system several times to make sure the enrollment process has been done correctly. After a few trials, the employee becomes comfortable with the system.

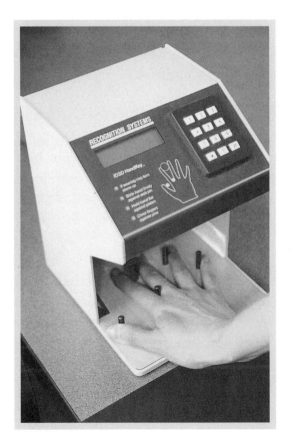

A hand scanner analyzes the physical features of a person's hand. A database stores a record of the features that are unique to that individual.

The hotel is very pleased with its new security system. It takes just 2 seconds to scan someone's hand, search the database, and decide whether the person is allowed to enter. This is less time than it took for an employee to enter a PIN and pass a card through a reader. More importantly, the hotel's money is much more secure.

This hotel is just one of the many businesses now using security systems that take advantage of *biometric traits*—unique, measurable physical or behavioral features that can be used to recognize or verify a person's identity.

Hand scanners are not the first devices that rely on *biometrics*—the study and analysis of biometric traits. Thousands of years ago, the ancient Egyptians measured people's hands and feet to identify them. The ancient Chinese analyzed the differences among people's fingers for identification purposes. But these measurements were often inaccurate and lacked the precision of modern-day biometrics.

The Beginning of Biometrics

Modern biometrics got off to a slow start. In 1684, a British doctor wrote a paper explaining that fingerprints vary among individuals. It wasn't until the mid-1800s that fingerprints were widely accepted as a reliable means of identifying individuals. Today, law-enforcement officials routinely use the swirls and ridges on people's fingertips as evidence in criminal cases.

Without the help of fingerprints, many crimes would never have been solved. One such crime became known as The Great Train Robbery. It occurred in England on August 8, 1963. That afternoon, a group of masked men robbed the Royal Mail train as it was traveling through the countryside on its way to London. In less than 15 minutes, the robbers made off with £2.5 million—more than $52 million in today's money. The Great Train Robbery was one of the most lucrative heists in history.

Have you ever seen a movie or a television show where the police fingerprint a suspect by rolling his or her fingers across an ink pad and then pressing them on a piece of paper? Did you wonder what your own fingerprints look like?

It's easy to find out. All you need is a soft-lead pencil, transparent tape, two pieces of white paper, and a hand lens. Trace the outline of your hand on one piece of paper. Cut five 1½-inch (3.8-cm) pieces of transparent tape, and rub the pencil lead on the second piece of paper. The lead, which is really a substance known as graphite, will serve as an ink pad. Rub the tip of one finger from the hand you traced on the pencil lead.

"Lift" the print by placing a piece of transparent tape along the length of your fingertip. Gently lift the tape from your finger and transfer the print to the corresponding finger on the drawing of your hand. Repeat the procedure with the other four fingers of your hand. Then wash your hands with soap and water to avoid smudging your prints.

Look at your fingerprints closely with a hand lens. Does each finger have the same pattern? Repeat the procedure using your other hand. Do the fingerprints on each thumb or each index finger match? Compare your fingerprints to a friend's? How similar are they? The chance of two individuals having the same fingerprint is less than one in a billion.

After the robbery, the thieves kept the stolen money at a small farmhouse while they planned their next move. Neighbors noticed the strangers, became suspicious, and called the police. When the police arrived, the robbers—and the money—were gone. But the thieves left

Police stand guard outside the farmhouse where the thieves involved in The Great Train Robbery hid out. Unfortunately, the robbers fled before police could capture them.

something behind—their fingerprints. Using this evidence, the police eventually arrested everyone involved in The Great Train Robbery. Unfortunately, most of the money was never recovered.

In other crimes, fingerprints are just one piece of the evidence used by law-enforcement officials. At 9:02 A.M. on April 19, 1995, a 4,800-pound (2,180-kg) bomb exploded outside the Alfred P. Murrah Federal Building in Oklahoma City, Oklahoma. The bomb killed 168 people.

When the bomb exploded, Marcial Escobedo, who had recently opened a Mexican cafe near the federal building, was standing next to a window. The window had bars on it to keep out burglars. The force of the blast shattered the window, sending pieces of glass in all

Shortly after the Alfred P. Murrah Federal Building in Oklahoma City blew up, rescue workers began searching for survivors.

directions. Smoke poured in through the bars. Escobedo later said that he "thought it was the end of the world."[1] Fortunately, he was not injured.

Ron White parked his car outside the nearby Fashion Cleaners Laundry shortly before the bomb exploded. When he heard the blast, White looked outside and "watched the top of the [federal] building just disappear. It was big chunks of debris twirling and shooting up in the air. It still doesn't seem real."[2] White was not hurt by the blast, but the hood of his car was dented by flying debris.

At the nearby Merkel X-Ray Company, the blast from the explosion blew several workers out of their chairs. Fortunately, no one was injured. The blast also blew open the doors of the local First Lutheran Church. When Steve Bittinger heard the explosion, he was on his hands and knees, cleaning a blackboard near the doors. He immediately rolled out of the way. Bittinger claims, "If I hadn't moved, I would have been maimed."[3]

On August 15, 1997—more than 2 years after the blast—Timothy McVeigh was sentenced to death for having detonated the bomb that killed 168 people. On June 5, 1998, Terry Nichols was sentenced to life imprisonment without any chance for parole. Nichols and McVeigh had planned the bombing together. Fingerprints helped convict both men.

No one actually saw McVeigh at the federal building on the day of the explosion. The evidence against him included the testimony of one of his closest friends, traces of explosives on several pieces of his clothing, and eyewitnesses who identified him as the person who rented the truck that transported the explosives used in the bombing. Investigators also found McVeigh's fingerprints on a receipt for 1 ton of fertilizer— the main ingredient used to make the bomb.

Nichols had told investigators that he had not seen McVeigh for months prior to the bombing, but a receipt found in his wallet proved that he was lying. The receipt was for an oil filter purchased from a Wal-Mart

Timothy McVeigh (left) and Terry Nichols (right) were convicted for their involvement in destroying the Federal Building in Oklahoma City.

store in Kansas. There were five fingerprints on the receipt—three belonged to Nichols, and two belonged to McVeigh. The date on the receipt showed that the two had been together shortly before the bombing.

The evidence used to convict McVeigh and Nichols was fairly traditional. Law enforcement officials have relied on eyewitness testimony and testing for gunpowder or explosives residue for many years. In recent years, however, scientists have developed many new kinds of tools—biometric tools—for catching criminals. Today, fingerprints are only one of the biometric tools used to catch criminals, and applications of biometric devices extend far beyond police departments and courtrooms.

In the last few decades, the development and use of biometric systems has mushroomed. As scientists discover additional traits that can be used to establish a person's identity, manufacturers of biometric systems have responded by developing new devices. Each year, biometric tools—fingerprint scanners, hand scanners, eye scanners, facial-recognition devices, voice-pattern-recognition devices, and signature-verification devices—become less expensive and more accurate.

Before taking a closer look at biometric traits and the devices used to recognize them, it is important that you understand why biometric traits vary from person to person. What makes you—and every other person on Earth—so unique? The answer to this question can be found within the *genes* that make up your *DNA*.

2 What Makes You Unique?

DNA (DEOXYRIBONUCLEIC ACID) is a molecule found in the *nucleus* of every cell in your body. It contains information about your *heredity*—the features you have inherited from your ancestors. DNA is located on rod-shaped structures called *chromosomes*. Nearly all of the cells in your body contain forty-six chromosomes.

Every molecule of DNA is made of small units called *nucleotides*. Each nucleotide contains a sugar, a phosphate, and a base. These units join together to create a DNA molecule shaped like a spiraling ladder. Scientists call this shape a *double helix*.

There are four kinds of bases in DNA—guanine (G), cytosine (C), thymine (T), and adenine (A). These nucleotide bases, which join together to form the rungs of the DNA ladder, carry instructions for making *amino acids*. A segment of DNA that carries all the information needed to string a group of amino acids into a protein is called a gene.

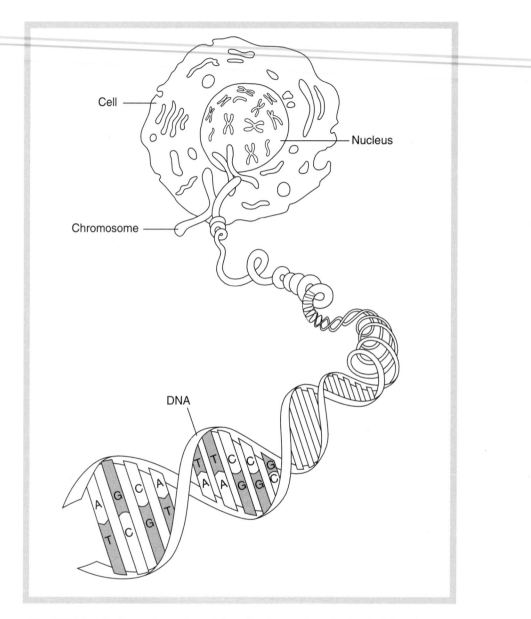

Cell

Nucleus

Chromosome

DNA

The DNA inside the nucleus of a cell has the shape of a spiraling ladder. Four kinds of bases, represented by the letters G, C, T and A, make up the rungs of the DNA ladder.

Because proteins are the chief building blocks of your cells, the instructions contained in your genes determine who you are—the color of your eyes and hair, the size of your brain, the shape of your hand, your blood type, the pitch of your voice, your talents and abilities, what diseases you may develop, and more. As you can see, DNA is a very important molecule.

A Look at Cell Division

You inherit your DNA from your parents. When a sperm cell from your father united with an egg cell from your mother, the resulting cell contained twenty-three chromosomes from each parent. As a result, the fertilized cell had a total of forty-six chromosomes. After about 30 hours, that first cell divided in half and became an *embryo.*

The cells of the embryo continued to divide by a process called *mitosis* and, about 9 months later, you were born. The cells in your body did not stop undergoing mitosis when you were born, however. That process will continue until the day you die.

An adult human consists of some 100 trillion cells. That's a big number! If someone handed you a dollar every second, it would take you more than 3 million years to accumulate $100 trillion!

During mitosis, each chromosome makes a copy of itself. The chromosomes line up along the middle of the cell. Each chromosome can take its place anywhere along this line—each is independent of the others. After they have lined up, each copy of a chromosome pair moves away from the other—toward opposite ends of the cell.

In this way, the original chromosome is parceled out to one of the new cells, and the copy ends up in the other new cell. As a result, each of the new cells has genetic information identical to that of the parent cell. Because the two new cells formed by mitosis have the same DNA and the same genes as their parent cell, this process is not responsible for a person's unique qualities. If all cell division occurred by mitosis,

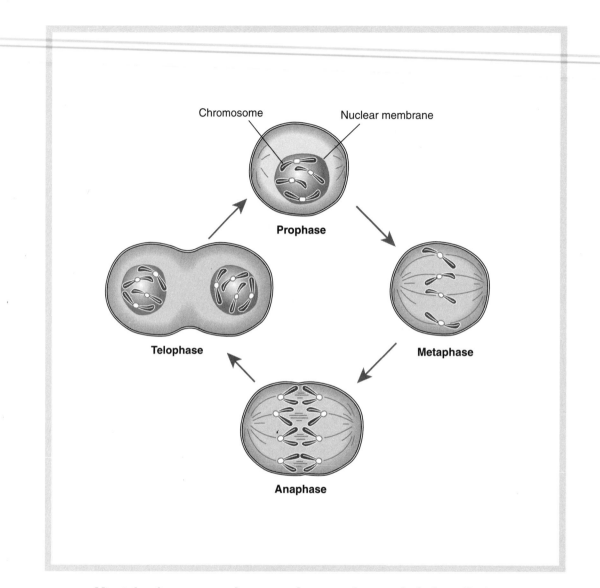

Mitosis has four steps–prophase, metaphase, anaphase, and telophase. During prophase, the nucleus begins to break down and chromosomes become visible. During metaphase, the chromosomes line up along in the middle of the cell. During anaphase, the chromosomes move toward the opposite ends of the cell. During telophase, the cell begins to split into two new cells. Each of the two cells has the same number and kinds of chromosomes as the original cell.

every person in the world would look almost exactly the same. Scientists realized that another kind of cell division must exist.

Another Kind of Cell Division

As scientists continued to study chromosomes, they came across yet another reason to search for a second kind of cell division. If eggs and sperm cells formed by mitosis, each one would have forty-six chromosomes.

By examining what happens to chromosomes when sex cells form, scientists discovered a kind of cell division called *meiosis*. During meiosis, the chromosome number is reduced by half. Meiosis occurs only when *gametes*—sperm and egg cells—mature in preparation for fertilization. All other cells undergo mitosis.

Because gametes have twenty-six chromosomes, fertilized egg cells end up with forty-six chromosomes. Thus, the number of chromosomes remains constant from one generation to the next.

During meiosis, chromosomes do not line up independently. Instead, the two chromosomes in each pair travel together. The pair may take a position at any point in the line of chromosomes that extends across the middle of the cell, but each chromosome in the pair must be opposite its partner.

Every time a male produces a sperm or a female produces an egg, there are 8,388,608 different ways in which the chromosomes can line up. Each of these possible arrangements will result in a person with different traits. While the chromosomes are paired, the partners may twist around each other. If this happens, the chromosomes may break and material that was originally part of one chromosome may end up attached to its partner. In this process, called *genetic recombination*, DNA is exchanged between the partners. The DNA swapping can take place at any point along the length of a chromosome. It can even occur at several places along the same chromosome.

Genetic recombination is the main reason that each person is unique. Each time a sperm or egg forms, the forty-six chromosomes are likely to pair up in a different arrangement. Moreover, the places at which they recombine are likely to be different. As a result, it is extremely unlikely that any two sperm or eggs produced by the same individual will be identical. Thus, no matter how many children a couple has, each child is unique.

Scientists estimate that the forty-six chromosomes in humans contain between 75,000 and 100,000 genes. Although these genes are not evenly divided among the chromosomes, each chromosome contains on average 1,600 to 2,200 genes.

With so many genes on a chromosome, the number of possible gene combinations that one individual can express is almost limitless. You should now recognize that, apart from identical twins—which form when a fertilized egg splits and develops into two separate individuals—the odds of two individuals having the same physical traits are practically zero.

3 Putting Biometrics to Work

POLICE DEPARTMENTS AROUND the world were the first to make widespread use of biometrics for identifying individuals. In the past few decades, however, the use of biometric traits has extended far beyond criminal investigations. The federal and state governments use biometrics for prison management, military security, border control, entitlement programs, and issuing drivers' licenses. It is also used by banks, amusement parks, and countless other corporations and organizations.

In 1996, approximately 10,000 biometric devices were in operation worldwide. By 2000, that number had escalated to more than 50,000. The biometrics industry expects to experience a 7.5 percent compound annual growth rate between the years 1996 and 2003.[1] Have you ever encountered a biometric device? They are used at many automated teller machines (ATMs), at the entrance of Walt Disney World, and at border patrol stations between the United States and Canada.

Biometric Systems Improve Banking

In March 1998, a United States senator introduced a bill that would authorize banks and other financial institutions to switch entirely to electronic fund-transfer systems. To complete a banking transaction, an individual would have to submit some form of biometric data, such as a fingerprint, or use a *smart card*—a wallet-size card that contains a microchip encoded with certain information about the individual.

In 1999, the Bank of America in San Francisco, California, launched a program allowing its employees to use smart cards to access on-line banking services. A microchip in their smart cards stores their on-line banking log-in identification number, a passcode, and a fingerprint.

To bank on-line, an employee logs on to the bank's Web page. The person then inserts his or her smart card into a portable reading device connected to the computer's disk drive. To complete the biometric identification process, an employee must place a finger on a small scanning device attached to the computer. The device compares the employee's fingerprint to the image stored on the smart card. If the two match, the system reads the employee's on-line banking identification number and passcode. At this point, the employee can securely carry out any banking transaction on-line.

To increase the security of financial transactions, many banks are looking for ways to replace PINs. Because they can be easily stolen or obtained, PINs do not provide as much security against theft as banks would like. Biometric technology is more secure because it is based on a physical trait that only one individual possesses.

Some banks have installed special cameras at their ATMs. When an individual inserts a bank card in the ATM, the camera photographs his or her eye. The photographic image is compared with an image stored in a central database. If the images match, the individual can use the ATM without entering a PIN. Some banks are also using de-

This scanner will compare this individual's fingerprint to the one stored on the smart card that is being swiped through the device. If the two match, then the individual is granted access to on-line banking services.

vices that scan other biometric traits, such as the features on an individual's hand.

Other financial institutions are also taking advantage of biometrics. Since 1997, a check-cashing company in Texas has cashed $100 million in checks at machines that photograph a user and compare the image to a photograph taken when the person opened his or her account. The user enters the amount of the check and places it in the designated slot. In less than a minute, the check is processed, and the individual gets the money.

Individuals can cash checks in this manner 24 hours a day, 7 days a week—as long as their photograph matches the one stored in the company's central database. The system is designed to account for slight differences in a person's facial appearance. For example, a person may wear glasses when the original photograph is taken, but later switch to contact lenses. If the system cannot make a match, it instructs the person to call a company representative. Before completing the transaction, the individual must answer questions based on the personal information provided when the account was established.

Biometric Systems Can Limit Physical Access

Biometric devices are also being used at Walt Disney World. A person who has an annual or seasonal pass no longer needs a photo identification card to enter the park. Instead, he or she places a finger into a scanner. If the person's identity is verified, the individual is allowed to enter.

Residents of the Marshall Field Garden Apartments in Chicago, Illinois, gain access to their building by using a scanner that analyzes certain biometric traits on their hands. Hand scans are also used by a company in Massachusetts to ensure that only parents are permitted into its day-care center to pick up their children. At the University of Georgia, a student's identity must be verified with a hand-scanning device before he or she can enter one of the university's all-you-can-eat dining halls.

Biometric systems that limit physical access are also used in prisons. According to the U.S. Justice Department, about 40 percent of the people who escape from federal prisons walk out the front door. What's their trick? Most simply pretend they are a visitor. To prevent such escapes, the government is installing hand-identification equipment. A visitor's identity must be verified by a hand scan before he or she is allowed to leave the prison.

The value of biometrics to restrict access has also been recognized by the International Olympic Committee. During the 1996 Summer Olympics in Atlanta, Georgia, access to the Olympic Village was

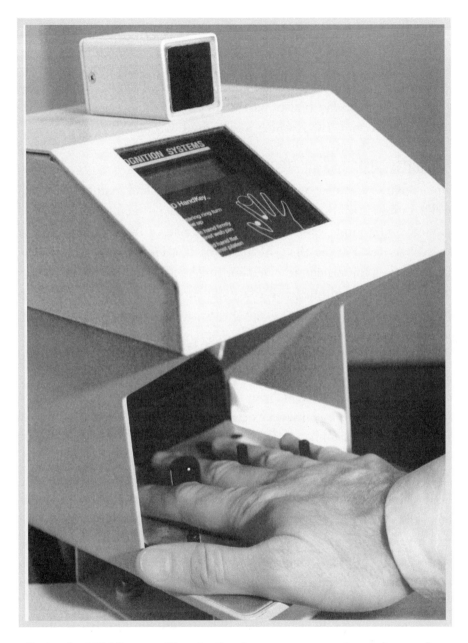

During the 1996 Summer Olympics, hand scanners were used to make sure that only authorized individuals were allowed into to the Olympic Village.

controlled with a hand scanner. The system verified the identity of 65,000 athletes, trainers, and support staff as they entered and left the Olympic Village.

During the 1998 Winter Olympics in Nagano, Japan, athletes competing in the biathlon had to pass through an iris scanner before they could retrieve their rifles, which were stored in a locked room.

Biometric Systems Can Prevent Fraud

On a cold November morning in 1998, a woman named Deborah walked into a social services office in Connecticut to collect her welfare money. As Deborah waited in line, the woman in front of her told the social services worker that she had lost her identification card. The worker asked the woman to place her finger in a scanner. Within a fraction of a second, an image of a face appeared on a monitor. Matching the woman's face with the image on the screen, the worker gave the woman her money.

Next came Deborah's turn. When Deborah placed her finger in the scanner, the office worker refused to give her any money. The scan had revealed that Deborah had been in the office before—under another name with another social security number and date of birth. Fortunately for Deborah, it was only a test. The company that installed the scanning system had asked her to test it.

The Connecticut Department of Social Services currently uses the fingerprint scanner to verify the identity of 85,000 people who are eligible for benefits. These people were chosen to field-test the system to see if it could reduce—or even eliminate—fraud. Since the program was started, the system has identified thirty-five cases of fraud. In one case, the system caught a person who had previously collected $10,000 by using two different identities.

Social services officials estimate that, in addition to catching thirty-five people, the system has also prevented an estimated 11,000 people from trying to beat the system. Before the biometrics system was

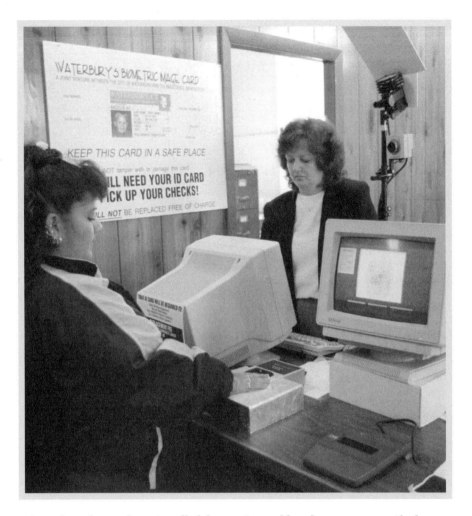

A number of states have installed fingerprint and hand scanners to verify the identity of individuals applying for social security benefits.

installed, these people had been able to steal with little fear of getting caught. Biometrics has saved the department—and taxpayers—more than $9 million.[2]

Social service offices in ten other states have installed similar bio-metric devices, and two other states—New York and New Jersey—are cross-matching their records to detect people trying to collect benefits in two or more states.

In West Virginia, the Department of Motor Vehicles is using biometrics as part of its licensing program. With approximately 1.3 million licensed drivers, the state issues about 450,000 driver's licenses and identification cards each year. Whenever a person seeks to renew a driver's license—or to replace a lost or stolen license—the system automatically compares a new photograph of the applicant with the image stored in a central database. The applicant is also asked to place a finger in a scanner so that the system can verify that too. A new license is issued only if a match is made. This system has significantly reduced the use of fake driver's licenses and identification cards in West Virginia.

The Immigration and Naturalization Service at John F. Kennedy Airport in New York and at Newark Airport in New Jersey also uses a biometric system to prevent fraud. Hand scanners and voice-recognition systems verify the identities of some 100,000 frequent visitors to the United States.

Similar systems have been installed at border patrol stations along the U.S.–Canadian border. People who frequently cross the border on business can obtain a smart card bearing their handprints and fingerprints. When crossing the border, they place the card and their hand in a scanner. If the images match, the traveler can pass through a special gate and avoid waiting in line.

Some businesses also rely on biometrics to eliminate fraud. Keeping track of employee attendance and work hours has always been a major problem for businesses. Time clocks are not a satisfactory solution because workers can easily check in for co-workers, a process known as "buddy punching." The largest supermarket chain in Australia uses fingerprint scanners to keep track of the attendance and work hours of its nearly 80,000 employees. In the United States, Coca-Cola uses hand scanners to prevent its workers from buddy punching.

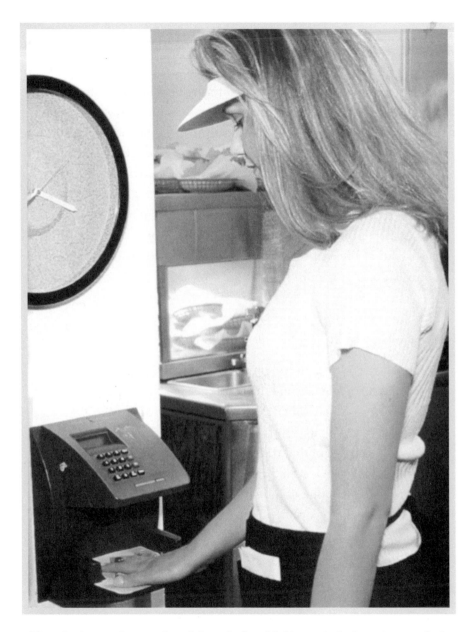

Many businesses have replaced time clocks with biometric devices. As a result, it is no longer possible for an employee to punch in for a co-worker who is late for his or her shift.

Biometric Systems Can Prevent Theft of Information

Have you ever bought something over the Internet? If so, you probably saw a screen that warned you about entering personal information, such as a credit card number. If this information falls into the wrong hands, it can be used illegally to make purchases or to get a cash advance. The Internet is not as secure as some people would like it to be.

In May 1997, Carlos Felipe Salgado Jr., was arrested by police in Daly City, California, for stealing information from the credit card accounts of 100,000 people. Salgado got this information by hacking into the database of an Internet service provider. When company officials discovered that their files had been infiltrated, they contacted the Federal Bureau of Investigation (FBI).

How Biometric Systems Work

All biometric systems have four stages: capture, extraction, comparison, and matching. During the capture stage, a biometric "sample" is taken from an individual. When a person enrolls in the system, he or she must submit several samples so that the system can build an average profile of that trait. For example, a person may be asked to place a finger in a scanner several times. Each scan is compared with the others. If one of the images is poor, the system will not use it to produce the record kept in the central database.

During the extraction stage, the system selects, or extracts, certain features of the biometric trait and converts them into a mathematical or digital code that resembles a bar code. This digital code is called a *reference template*. Some biometric systems require that the template be connected to other data. For example, the system may ask an individual to enter a PIN or insert a smart card that holds the template.

To track down the thief, the FBI enlisted the help of a civilian who eventually established an on-line contact with Salgado. Using the Internet, Salgado sold the person 710 credit card numbers for $710 and another 580 numbers for $2,900. (Salgado charged more for the second batch of credit card numbers because their cash limits were much higher than those of the first batch.)

The FBI then decided it was time to move in on Salgado. They set up a meeting between Salgado and an undercover agent. Salgado was arrested as he tried to sell a CD-ROM with 100,000 names and credit card numbers to the agent for $260,000.

"We had determined that he was in the market to sell this information," said FBI spokesman George Grotz, "and we were able to contact him via the Internet and set up a meeting to discuss the terms of the

Each time the individual uses the system, a new profile is compiled and compared to the reference template. During the matching stage, the system may evaluate the similarity between the new sample and the reference template. This is called a "one-to-many" match.

If a match is made, the person has been recognized as having one of the many templates stored in the database. In effect, the system has answered the question "Does this person match one in our files?"

If the system has been designed to search for a connection between the reference template and a particular individual, the device will decide whether the new profile matches the person who has entered the PIN or inserted the smart card. This is called a "one-to-one" match. In this case, the system answers the question "Is this person really who he or she claims to be?"

A biometric device, such as a finger scanner, can be used to limit access to information stored in a computer database.

sale. We believe that he has been hacking into various protected computers for at least 5 years."[3] Three months after his arrest, Salgado pleaded guilty to 4 felony counts and was sentenced to 30 years in prison and a $1-million fine.

Theft of computer information is a rapidly growing concern. The value of information that is stolen through computer theft and loss is currently estimated at more than $800 million a year.[4] And that figure is expected to rise. How can such crimes be stopped? Biometric devices are one possibility. According to George Wells, president of Digital Biometrics, "You need to be sure that people seeking access to information are who they say they are and [that] they have the right to access that information."[5] Verifying identity is becoming increasingly important as computer transactions replace personal transactions.

In May 1999, SAC Technologies released a software program that allows a user to create a separate password to access each program file, program, and directory. The software, which sells for $14.95, is used in conjunction with SAC Technologies' biometric fingerprint identification system. According to company officials, the combined software and biometric system "offers a total security solution."[6] Only time will tell if hackers like Salgado will find a way to get around this new system.

Can Biometric Systems Make Mistakes?

A biometric system will either match or not match the new information it extracts with the data stored as a reference template. Like any system, biometric systems are not completely error-free. In some cases, an individual may be rejected by mistake. In other cases, an individual may be accepted by mistake.

Several factors can affect how well a system manages to avoid *false rejections* and *false acceptances*. Environmental conditions, such as extreme temperatures or high humidity, can affect a system's performance. Physical conditions, such as dirt on an individual's hands, can affect the user's performance. A user's performance can also be jeopardized if the person is not comfortable using the system. For this reason, training people to use the system correctly is extremely important.

For systems where security is the primary concern, a false acceptance can be disastrous. A biometric system would not be doing its job if it granted the wrong person access to a bank's main vault, for example. To minimize such occurrences, the system can be designed so that its false acceptance rate is as low as 0.001 percent. Such a system would issue a false acceptance in only 1 in 100,000 cases. If an average of 10 people entered the main vault each day, then a false acceptance may occur once every 38 years. By putting biometrics to work, the odds of an unauthorized person gaining access to the vault would be quite small.

4 The Hand as a Biometric Tool

AT PRESENT, NEARLY 150 biometric identification systems are available for sale. These systems can be divided into two categories: those that evaluate physical traits, such as fingerprints, hand geometry, and facial features, and those that assess behavioral traits, such as handwriting and voice patterns.

Systems that analyze fingerprints and hand geometry are the most popular. Many users feel uncomfortable interacting with a device that scans their eye or takes their photograph. They would rather have their finger or hand scanned. Because biometric systems that include finger and hand scans are quickly becoming more affordable, they are more attractive to small businesses.

Fingerprint Scanners

Every month, fingerprint matches help law-enforcement officers apprehend more than 2,700 fugitives.[1] When a suspect is brought into custody, police often take a set of fingerprints.

These may be sent to the FBI to see if the suspect has a criminal history or is wanted in connection with other crimes. Law-enforcement officers are interested in fingerprint scanners because they can be used in conjunction with the FBI's massive fingerprint database, which contains 214 million fingerprint cards representing 74 million individuals.

This police officer is scanning the finger of a suspect arrested at the city jail in Santa Ana, California.

The FBI's fingerprint database was originally stored as images on paper, but it is currently being converted into mathematical codes and stored in an electronic database. When the FBI's Integrated Automated Fingerprint Identification System is up and running, a police officer anywhere in the United States will be able to get results in just 24 hours. In the past, the matching process took as long as 10 weeks.

Fingerprint scanners are highly accurate, easy to use, and involve a biometric trait that will not change over time. Most finger-scanning systems capture, extract, and compare the small unique marks that are left when a finger comes into contact with a surface. These marks are called *minutiae*. Each one represents a point where two ridges on a fingertip meet. A fingerprint normally contains up to 100 of these points.

Some fingerprint scanners analyze the tiny sweat pores between these points. No two individuals have the same pattern of sweat pores on their fingertips. Other fingerprint scanners analyze the distance between these points.

Law-enforcement agencies are not the only ones interested in fingerprint scanners. These devices are also used to license drivers, to keep track of employees' work hours, to control access to ATMs and on-line banking services, to monitor individuals traveling across the border between the United States and Canada, and to limit access to patient files at hospitals and other health-care facilities.

O'Hare International Airport in Chicago, Illinois, is the busiest airport in the United States, with about 250,000 passengers flying in or out each day. Like other airports, O'Hare has increased its security over the past several years in response to terrorists' threats. Before boarding a plane, passengers are asked a series of questions, and they must pass through a metal detector and show a photo ID. Officials at O'Hare have recently taken steps to tighten security even more. They are now using fingerprint scanners to monitor something that passengers rarely see—air cargo.

According to Mary Rose Loney, aviation commissioner of Chicago, about 60 percent of all air-cargo shipments that pass through O'Hare are transported on passenger planes. Cargo that passes through an airport may be an easy target for a terrorist planning to conceal a bomb on board a plane.

In most airports, when a truck driver delivers cargo, all the driver needs to gain access is a written manifest and a photocopy of his or her driver's license. However, in early 1994, a representative of the trucking industry approached Richard Kunicki, Chicago's deputy aviation commissioner, with an interesting request. He asked Kunicki to explore the possibility of developing an air cargo security system jointly with the airport, the airlines, and the Federal Aviation Agency. "[The trucking industry] wanted to make sure that they have done everything humanly possible to secure that cargo," says Kunicki.[2]

Working with the trucking companies and the airlines, O'Hare officials developed a biometric package that allows them to verify the identity of any driver authorized to make a delivery at the airport. The package includes a fingerprint scanner. Nearly 700 truck drivers who routinely deliver cargo to O'Hare voluntarily enrolled in the biometric system. Identix Corporation then set up fingerprint scanners at twenty-four locations throughout the airport.

Today, a truck driver arriving at O'Hare is instructed to insert a smart card into a reader. An image similar to that found on a driver's license appears on a screen. The image has the driver's name, photo, and employer information. The driver then places a finger in a scanner to verify that the card belongs to the driver. If the driver's identity is verified, then a screen describing the cargo's contents appears. In addition, several sets of numbers are shown on the screen. One set, known as the seal number, must match the one that has been placed by the shipper on the truck. If all the numbers match, the driver is allowed into the airport.

While no biometric system will be able to deter all terrorists or thieves, the system can be used as an instant investigative tool if a breach of security occurs. Within minutes of a terrorist act, the plane's cargo can be traced from the airport, back to the driver, and then to the shipper. By retracing the steps the cargo followed in its trip to the airport, investigators may be able to find out who planted the bomb.

In the future, fingerprint scanners may even be used to identify missing children. In the United States, more than 2,000 children get lost, are abducted, or run away every day. Nearly 750,000 are reported missing every year—that's about one child every 18 seconds.[3]

Finding a missing child can be a daunting task. The longer a child is missing, the more his or her physical appearance will change. After a few years, photos of the child may be useless. But fingerprints never change. If law-enforcement officers have a copy of the missing child's fingerprints, proving his or her identity will be much easier.

For these reasons, many police departments encourage citizens in their communities to have their children fingerprinted. It is now possible for parents to buy inexpensive home fingerprinting kits that are easy to use and produce a reliable set of fingerprints. The fingerprints can be filed with a local law-enforcement agency and may even be converted to electronic fingerprints and added to the FBI's databank.

Although reliable and accurate, fingerprint scanners are not ideal for every situation. For example, people working in settings where ink can easily get on their hands would not be suitable candidates to screen with a fingerprint scanner. Differences in age, gender, and ethnic background can also affect the quality of a scan.

Hand Scanners

The first hand-scanning devices, designed in the 1960s, were used to limit access to the control rooms of nuclear power plants. By the late 1960s, similar hand-scanning systems were being used in a few private companies. These early scanners evaluated hand geometry—the three-dimensional image that is formed by the entire hand. Hand geometry is not a reliable biometric trait—about 1 in 50 people have hand geometries similar enough to fool the scanners. Nevertheless, scanners that analyze hand geometry are useful for controlling access to a building with a limited number of occupants.

As biometrics technology has advanced, scientists have developed hand scanners that evaluate more reliable biometric traits. The new generation of hand scanners, which read the shape, size, and other features of a person's hand, have become the most popular commercially used biometric device.

Unlike fingerprints, handprints change over time. But certain features of a person's hands remain constant enough to be used as biometric traits. For example, the human palm has 10,000 points of information that a hand scanner can analyze. The three-dimensional shape of a person's fingers can also be used for identification, and so can the contour of an individual's knuckles when he or she makes a fist. When a person grips and turns a handle, the knuckles form a distinctive pattern that can be scanned.

Hand scanners are fast, user-friendly, and highly accurate. During an 18-month test period, hand scanners used by Sandia Laboratories in Albuquerque, New Mexico, had a false acceptance rate of 0.00025 percent. Such a device is expected to grant access to an unauthorized person only once for every 25 million people seeking entry.

In 1992, New York University in New York City installed two hand scanners to control access to one of its dormitories. In the past, the dormitory, which houses more than 1,000 students, always had lines of students waiting to have their photo IDs verified before they could enter. Now students no longer have to wait in line or worry about losing their ID card. The hand scanners have also eliminated the fraudulent use of photo IDs to gain access to the dormitory.

A hand-scanning biometric system called INSPASS is currently being used at the customs checkpoints of six international airports in the United States. To use the system, a person inserts a card into an INSPASS booth. The system reads the ID number on the card and sends

The INSPASS system is used to process people traveling through airports. The system takes less than a minute to verify an individual's identity. People not enrolled in the system may wait several hours to be cleared by workers.

the information to a central database run by the U.S. Customs Service. The database pulls up the hand template that corresponds to that card. When the system is ready, a green light flashes and the person places his or her right hand on a reflective surface. A camera takes a geometric image of the hand, and the system compares the new image to the one in the database. If the images match, the person is allowed to pass through customs.

This entire process takes less than 1 minute. Because checking identities of international travelers without the use of a biometric system can take up to 3 hours, more than 71,000 people have already enrolled in the program. As an additional incentive, U.S. and Canadian citizens who fly overseas on business at least three times a year can enroll free of charge.

Some recently developed security systems include a hand scanner used in conjunction with a fingerprint scanner. In such a system, a hand scanner is used to control access to a building. Within the

Designing a More Reliable Hand Scanner

Researchers at Michigan State University are trying to develop a more precise hand scanner. Their system consists of a light source, a camera, a mirror, and a flat surface containing five precisely positioned pegs. The five pegs ensure that the user's hand is correctly positioned before it is scanned. The mirror projects a sideview of the user's hand into the camera. To determine whether a user's hand matches one in the database, the system measures the width and length of the fingers. Perhaps this system will someday be used to restrict access to sensitive data on the World Wide Web. Scientists are testing a prototype that uses hand scans to verify the identity of users before they can access certain Web pages. Such a system eliminates the need for passwords.

building, fingerprint scanners may be installed at various locations where a greater degree of security is required. For example, in a company with 1,000 employees, everyone may be required to pass through a hand scanner at the building's main entrance. Of those 1,000 employees, only 10 may be approved by a finger scanner to access the vault where the cash is kept.

5 The Eyes and Face as Biometric Tools

IN THE LATE 1980s, officials at the Cook County Sheriff's Office in Chicago, Illinois, initiated a program to prevent prisoners from escaping by pretending to be a visitor, an employee, or a released prisoner. The prisons needed a biometric system with a very high accuracy rate. In other words, the number of both false acceptances and false rejections had to be extremely low. Only then could they be confident that the right person was being allowed to leave.

The sheriff's office chose a system that uses the eye as a biometric tool because a person's eye contains two structures that provide a very high level of accuracy whenever they are scanned—the *retina* and the *iris*. The retina is the light-sensitive inner layer of the eye. When light reaches the retina, it stimulates receptor cells called rods and cones. Rods are extremely sensitive to light and can detect various shades of gray even in dim light. Cones can detect colors and are important for seeing in bright light.

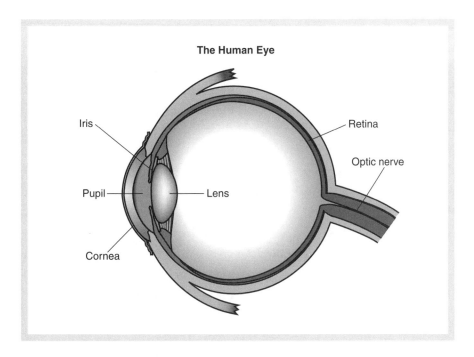

The Human Eye

The cornea is tough, transparent, and curved. It protects the rest of the eye. The iris is a colored ring that surrounds the pupil, which is located in front of the lens. The retina is a layer of tissue inside the eye that captures light. The optic nerve carries messages to the brain.

The iris is the colored ring that surrounds the pupil. Muscles in the iris control the size of the pupil and determine how much light can enter. When little light is available, the muscles in the iris enlarge the size of the pupil so that more light can enter the eye. In bright light, the muscles make the pupil smaller.

In October 1990, biometric systems that included an eye scanner were installed in Cook county's ten jails. After a suspect is arrested and booked at a Chicago police stations, he or she is transported to one of these jails to await a bail hearing. Shortly after arriving, the prisoner is processed. The person's eyes are scanned by a biometric device and a reference template is created.

The template is linked to a record of the criminal charges and personal information about the prisoner, such as gang membership and medical history. The prisoner's file is then added to the county's database, which currently contains information about approximately 350,000 individuals. The new file is checked against other files already in the database and against state and FBI databases to find out if the prisoner is wanted for other crimes.

Before a prisoner is released from the county jail, his or her identity must be verified by an eye scanner. During the first 6 months of 1991, the eye-scanning system caught 40 prisoners attempting to escape by using a false identity. The system is working so well that the county sheriff's office recently installed an eye scanner outside its computer center. Before entering, an employee must place one eye in a scanner. If the scan matches a record in the database, the door unlocks.

Retinal Scanning

The retina contains more than just rods and cones. It also contains many tiny *capillaries*—blood vessels that connect arteries and veins. Capillaries in the retina form a distinct pattern that can be used as a biometric trait. No two individuals—not even identical twins—share the same retinal capillary pattern. As a result, retinal scans have a very high rate of accuracy.

During a retinal scan, the user must insert one eye into a device. The eye must be about 3 inches (7.6 cm) from the eyepiece. In some cases, the user is asked to look through the eyepiece and focus on a green dot for a few seconds before the retina is scanned. In other cases, the user focuses on a target made up of several circles. When all the circles appear to overlap, the retina is scanned.

During the scan, infrared light illuminates the capillaries and the device captures an image of their pattern. The position of each blood vessel is mapped by the scanning system, and the information is

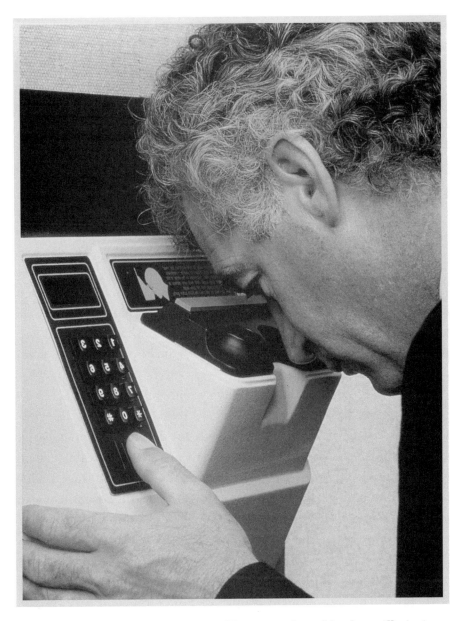

A retinal scanner captures an image of the pattern formed by the capillaries in the retina of a person's eye.

extracted and processed into a mathematical code that forms the reference template.

Although retinal scanners have a high rate of accuracy when used correctly, they also have some disadvantages. They cannot be used by people who are blind or who have cataracts. More importantly, they are not as user-friendly as most other biometric devices. Many people are reluctant to place an eye in the device and feel uneasy about having an infrared beam projected into their eye—even though they are assured that the light will not cause any damage.

A retinal scanner also requires a trained operator to help the users interact properly with the system. But even a well-trained operator cannot be sure that a user has correctly focused his or her eye. For this reason, retinal-scanning systems are prone to human error.

The Cook County Sheriff's Office is not the only Illinois government agency interested in retinal-scanning systems. The Illinois Human Services Department conducted a study to determine which of two biometric systems—electronic fingerprinting or retinal scanning—was more effective in detecting welfare fraud.

The department's retinal-scanning system creates a reference template by taking 320 readings of a person's retinal capillaries. The template is stored in a databank, along with the individual's photograph and identification information. The entire process of enrollment and identification with the retinal scanner normally takes less than 3 minutes. Only an individual whose identity is verified by a retinal scan can receive his or her welfare benefits. Anyone who refuses to cooperate may be removed from the welfare rolls.

Since the retinal-scanning project began in 1996, 7,800 people have enrolled. Although the finger-imaging part of the study began a year later, more than twice as many people are now enrolled in it. According to Barry Beckwith, chief of the Bureau of Operations Support for the Illinois Department of Human Services, "Finger imaging is more accurate in finding multiple enrollments. Retinal scanning is not client- or staff-friendly and requires considerable time to secure biometric records."[1] Based on this 2-year study, the Illinois Department of Human Services ended the retinal-scanning project in July 1998, but is continuing with the finger-imaging project.

Other groups who have tested retinal scans report the same findings. Because they are not staff- or user-friendly, agencies and businesses have looked for a more suitable biometric system. Perhaps retinal scans will find their niche in places where the users have no choice—like the Cook County jails. Here retinal scans have been warmly received by officials. Cook County Sheriff Michael Sheahan says, "We believe the system will put us on the cutting edge and develop into a national model."[2]

Since Cook County began its retinal-scanning program of prisoners, it has received $10.3 million from the U.S. Department of Justice to expand the system. In addition, 103 surrounding suburban communities have each given Cook County $20,000 to support the program.

Iris Scanning

An iris scanner is the best choice for verifying identity because no two people have identical irises. In fact, the two irises of a single individual are unique. The iris is a better biometric tool than fingers, hands, and even retinas because it has thousands of measurable features that can be captured, extracted, and used to form a reference template. Because the iris has more measurable features than any other body part, the resulting reference template is more complex. As a result, false acceptances and false rejections are extremely unlikely. Thus, an iris scanner is more accurate in verifying a person's identity than any other biometric system.

An iris scanner is also more user-friendly than a retinal scanner. Users look into a camera rather than placing one eye in a device, and no infrared beam is involved. In addition, an iris scanner makes a decision more quickly than a retinal scanner.

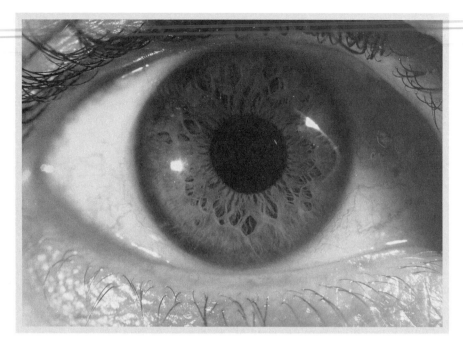

The iris is the colored part of the eye that surrounds the pupil. What color is your iris?

An ophthalmologist named Leonard Flom was the first person to recognize the value of the iris as a biometric tool. In 1987, he joined forces with another ophthalmologist named Aran Safir and a computer scientist named John Daugman. The three men developed the first commercial biometric system to use an iris scan. In 1994, they received a patent for their system.

To use an iris-scanning system, a person looks into a camera. The camera produces a black-and-white video image of the iris. The system extracts information from the pattern, converts it into a mathematic code, and compares it to the reference template stored in a database. The chances of an iris scan creating the same template from two different individuals is about 1 in 10^{78}.[3] This number is far larger than the

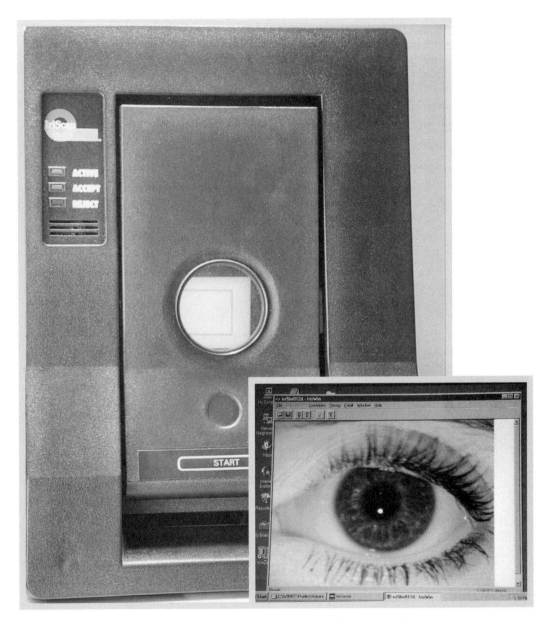

An iris scanner includes a camera (above) that captures a black-and-white image of the eye. The images are displayed on a computer screen (below).

Earth's human population. It is no wonder that no other biometric system can provide the same level of accuracy as an iris scanner.

Since it was first developed, the iris scanner has been modified and improved in a number of ways. New devices can detect muscle movements within the iris. These muscles are constantly expanding and contracting as light conditions change. This allows the system to distinguish between the iris of a living person and an artificial iris. As a result, a user cannot fool the system.

New devices also accommodate individuals who wear eyeglasses or contact lenses, but they will not operate properly if the eyeglasses are heavily scratched. The scratches can distort the image captured by the scanner.

Iris scanners are currently growing in popularity. Three international banks have recently announced that they will begin a test to evaluate how well iris scans verify the identity of their ATM customers. These banks—located in Italy, Norway, and Turkey—will use a system consisting of three cameras. Each one will zoom in on a customer as he or she walks up to an ATM.

One of the cameras will focus on the person's body, the second on the person's head, and the third on one of the person's eyes. This third camera can detect a human eye from 12 to 36 inches (30 to 91 cm) away. When all three cameras have captured an image of the individual, the camera focused on the eye zooms in for an iris scan. If a match is made, the person is allowed to use the ATM without entering a PIN. The entire process takes only a few seconds.

Some banks are also considering using iris scans to eliminate check fraud. The FBI estimates that banks and other financial institutions lose $12 billion to $15 billion each year because people successfully cash "bad" checks. If bank tellers used an iris scan to verify a person's identity before cashing a check, check fraud would be greatly reduced.

On May 18, 1999, Bank United of Houston, Texas, announced that it would install the country's first Iris Recognition ATM. Customers in selected branches in the Houston, Dallas, and Forth Worth areas are now able to withdraw cash from their accounts just by looking into a camera.

Bank United hopes that eventually Iris Recognition ATMs will be available at all its branches. To use the system, all a customer has to do is insert his or her ATM card into the machine and look into a camera. The camera instantly photographs the person's iris. If a match is found, the transaction is approved. This system has the ability to capture an iris image through eyeglasses, contact lenses, and most sunglasses.

Humans are not the only living things whose identities are being verified by iris scans. This technology is now being used on race horses. Because race horses are very expensive, and horse theft is not uncommon, some owners are protecting their investment by using an iris scanning system to create a reference template of their animal. If the horse is stolen and later found, its identity can be verified by comparing a new iris scan to the reference template.

At a recent national meeting, farmers expressed their concern about the growing incidence of farm-animal theft. A program that will test iris scanning on cattle is currently underway. If these scanners can be used to verify the identity of cows, farmers will be better able to protect their herd. Imagine how cattle rustlers in the Old West would have reacted to an iris scan!

Facial Recognition

After about 25 years of research, the human face is beginning to emerge as another useful biometric tool. After an image of a person's face is captured by a video camera, a biometric device extracts the information needed to form a reference template. Comparing the template to one stored in a database will result in either a match or a non-match. One major advantage of facial recognition devices is that they require little or no cooperation from the individual being evaluated.

Facial recognition is the most user-friendly kind of biometric system.

At first glance, you may think facial recognition is easy. After all, you never have trouble recognizing someone you know. But you might have a problem if you have not seen the person in a long time or if the person's appearance has changed in some way. For example, the person may have a new hairstyle, may be wearing glasses instead of contact lenses, or may have grown a beard. Establishing someone's identity using facial recognition is not as easy as it may seem.

Two main techniques are used for facial recognition. One was developed and patented by scientists at the Massachusetts Institute of Technology in Boston, Massachusetts. It involves capturing a facial image that is then mapped into a series of 128 numbers known as coefficients. These coefficients are used to form an *eigenface*–a two-dimensional arrangement of light and dark areas that represent an image of a face. To identify a face, this system compares the eigenface to images stored in its database. The entire process takes only 3 seconds.

A second approach to facial recognition is known as a *facial thermogram*–an image created by an infrared camera that can detect heat released from blood vessels beneath the skin. Like the blood vessels in the retina, the vessels beneath the skin of the face form a distinct pattern that can be used by a facial-recognition system. Facial thermograms can even be used to distinguish between identical twins.

Growing Use of Facial Recognition

Because it is easy to capture a facial image with a video camera, facial recognition is rapidly gaining popularity. This type of system is used by the Departments of Motor Vehicles in West Virginia and six other states. The system, designed and developed by Polaroid, uses a digital camera to take a picture of individuals when they apply for, renew, or seek a replacement for a lost driver's license.

When a person applies for a license for the first time, a copy of the digital photograph is placed on the license. The license is then laminated to form a bond with the photograph. Any tampering with the license to alter or replace the photograph renders it invalid. When a person tries to renew a license or replace a lost license, he or she will receive a new license on the spot if the image on the license matches the one stored in the database.

The biometric system is designed to ignore natural variations in skin tone. For example, a person's original license may have been issued in the winter but lost in the summer, when the individual's face may be quite tanned. The system also ignores differences in facial expressions and hair styles. The system has only one drawback—it may not be accurate in cases where a man has either grown or shaved off a beard.

To get around such a potential problem, the manufacturer has designed the system so that the operator must specify whether the applicant is bearded or not. When the system does not come up with a match, it will display the original picture to allow the human operator to make a final decision. According to Richard Grimm, manager of the West Virginia program for Polaroid, "Since the system was installed, the department has had an extremely low error rate."[4]

Jane Cline, West Virginia's Motor Vehicle Commissioner, feels that her department's facial-recognition system will prevent people from obtaining a driver's license under false pretenses. Cline says, "We are delighted to be the first [state] to provide facial recognition technology to this application. The West Virginia Department of Motor Vehicles clearly was forward-thinking in planning to utilize this security feature, and we're proud to be selected to provide this leading-edge technology."[5]

Databanks of facial images are growing rapidly. A.C. Nielsen, the television-rating company, has recently applied for a patent on a system that can photograph a customer's face while he or she is waiting in a checkout line. The image and a list of what the person has purchased can then be added to a database. Each time that person is photographed in line, the newly purchased items will be added to the database. The information can then be used to determine what products the individual is most likely to buy if contacted by phone or mail.

Databases of facial images can be given away, sold, or even networked to create a super database. Visage Technology in Littleton, Massachusetts, already has 45 million faces stored in its database. The next step would be to add personal information to each of those stored images.

For example, information about an individual's spending habits and recreational interests could be added. Such information would be valuable to anyone with something to sell. This stockpiling of personal information is one reason that some people are concerned about biometrics technology. You will examine some of these concerns in Chapter 8, but first, you'll take a brief look at behavioral traits that can be used as biometric tools.

6 Behavioral Traits as Biometric Tools

WITH THE HELP of a biometric system recently installed at Bermuda International Airport, some visitors no longer have to wait in line to pass through immigration. These travelers can use a credit card or debit card to enroll in a system known as Fastgate. Along with their card, travelers must also supply some personal information, including their home address, date of birth, and passport number. To complete the enrollment process, an individual must register a biometric trait, such as a fingerprint or handprint, that will be scanned whenever he or she arrives at the airport.

The traveler is then issued a card that contains encoded information, including the biometric data extracted from his or her scan. Once enrolled, a visitor simply inserts the card into a reader whenever he or she passes through immigration. While the individual answers some questions on a touch screen, the system is hard at work comparing the information on the card to what is stored in a database. Fastgate verifies the identity of the visitor and also checks with a border control database to make sure that no security alerts have been issued for the visitor. With the help of biometrics, the visitor is cleared through immigration in less than 15 seconds.

Voice Pattern: Physical or Behavioral Trait?

Rather than using a fingerprint or handprint to enroll in Fastgate, an individual can submit his or her voice pattern. A voice pattern consists of the sounds produced when air is forced past the vocal cords. The vocal cords consist of two ligaments that stretch across the *larynx*, or voice box. The pitch and volume of the sound depends on the amount of tension on the vocal cords and on the amount of air forced past them. The length of the neck, the size of the nasal chambers, and the shape of the mouth also affect the sound produced. The different pitches and volumes produced generate a voice pattern that is unique to each individual.

Some people working in the field of biometric technology think of voice pattern as a physical trait. After all, they argue, a person's voice pattern depends on the ligaments that make up the vocal cords. Others consider voice pattern to be a behavioral trait. They point out that a person's voice pattern is influenced by mood and frame of mind. Voice pattern is also affected by the geographic area in which a person grows up. For example, someone who was born and raised in Georgia will sound different from a person born and raised in New York.

Speech Recognition versus Voice Verification

Voice patterns are used by two different kinds of commercial voice systems: *speech-recognition* systems and *voice-verification* systems. Speech-recognition systems are used by people who would rather dictate than write. A number of software products are available that convert spoken words into written text. These products are designed to identify what a person is saying, but they are not capable of determining who said the words. Speech-recognition systems do not use the four steps employed by a biometric system—capture, extraction, comparison, and matching.

In contrast, voice-verification systems are used to verify an individual's identity. Fastgate uses this kind of system to move some visitors through immigration in less than 15 seconds. If a person decides to register his or her voice as a biometric trait in Fastgate, the individual must provide a sample of his or her voice pattern. Usually, the individual is asked to read a specially selected combination of phrases, words, and numbers. In other cases, the individual can say whatever he or she wishes to say. No matter which process is used, the person is usually asked to repeat what is said a number of times. In this way, the biometric system can build a profile of that person's voice pattern.

After the profile has been assembled, the system extracts the information needed to form a reference template that is stored in a database. The template of a voice pattern that is stored in a database is called a *voice print*. If the spoken input matches the voice print, then the person is declared a match.

Voice systems are usually designed for a "one-to-one" match. In other words, the system is designed to verify a person's identity. If a person has enrolled correctly and has established a good voice print, the system will rarely give either a false acceptance or false rejection. When it does, it is often because the person has a cold, laryngitis, or some other factor that is affecting his or her voice.

Accuracy is not the only advantage of voice-verification systems. They are also relatively inexpensive, costing about the same as a fingerprint scanner. But purchasing a voice-verification system may not even be necessary. Most personal computers now come with sound cards and simple microphones. If a company has this equipment, all it needs is software designed for voice verification. Voice-verification systems are also popular because they can make use of the global network of telephone lines and satellites. Unlike other biometric systems, voice verification does not require an individual to be within a certain distance of the scanning device. In fact, he or she can be hundreds or even thousands of miles away.

Using Voice Verification

Chase Manhattan Bank recently became the first financial institution to use voice verification to identify customers. The bank chose voice verification over other biometric systems because their customers preferred it. A market research study showed that 95 percent of consumers felt it was not intrusive. Customers also liked the system because it allowed them to access their accounts by phone.

To use the system, bank customers must enroll by reading a selected phrase either at a local branch or from home, over a telephone. The system then makes a voice print of the customer's voice pattern. When customers go to a local branch, they simply swipe their bank card through a reader and say the phrase they originally entered. If a match is made, they are given a receipt to present to a bank teller.

Voice verification is also being used to restrict access to programs that are stored on personal or laptop computers. For just $60, an individual can buy software and a microphone that will record the person's voice and establish a voice print. From that point on, a user will be allowed to access the programs, files, and folders on the computer only if his or her voice print matches the one stored in the computer's memory.

A user who happens to develop a cold or laryngitis can use a "back-door password" to access the protected data. The software also allows users to create multiple voice prints so that several people can read and use the programs and files stored on a single computer.

Access to computer networks can also be controlled by means of voice verification. Some networks have been set up so that a person enrolls by calling in and entering a previously assigned PIN. The person is then asked to enter his or her name and follow prompts that ask the individual to repeat a series of phrases or a series of two-digit numbers.

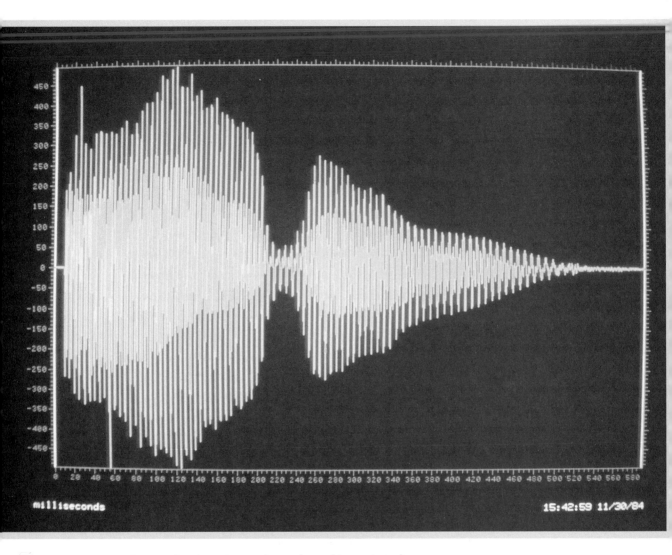

A person's voice print can be used as a biometric tool.

After a voice print has been made, the person is given a password and PIN to access the network. From that point on, the person simply calls in, enters his or her PIN, and says the password. If the system verifies the individual's voice, he or she can access the network.

Each day, millions of people use a telephone calling card to place a call or check their bank balance by telephone. In each case, the consumer cannot be absolutely sure that the line is secure. Telephone calling-card fraud is a serious problem. In 1995, one in six calling-card users in the United States were victims of fraud. The losses they sustained amount to $1 billion.[1]

In most cases, calling-card numbers are stolen by people who loiter around public telephones, especially in airports, railway stations, and hotel lobbies. They obtain PIN codes by watching people place telephone calls. These thieves may either use the stolen PIN code to make calls themselves, or they may sell them.

Stealing calling-card numbers affects people in countries all over the world. As a result, several European countries are currently testing a system that uses voice verification to approve telephone transactions. The system is so precise that it will reject a tape of the legitimate cardholder's voice.

Dynamic Signature Verification

A person's signature is often used as a means of identification. For example, salespeople routinely check a person's signature on a receipt against the one on the back of a credit card to verify the identity of the individual making the purchase. But a signature can be forged without too much effort. In some cases, the forgery can even fool experts.

Consider the case of a historical-document dealer who was caught forging the signatures of Billy the Kid, Butch Cassidy, Geronimo, Wyatt Earp, and other well-known figures from the Old West. Any one of these signatures, if genuine, is quite valuable. For example, an authentic document or letter signed by Wyatt Earp could bring as much as $20,000 at an autograph auction.

A number of papers allegedly signed by Earp have been sold at auction over the years. The signatures on these documents were verified as genuine by several autograph dealers. But careful examination by a handwriting expert familiar with Earp's life recently revealed that some of the signatures were forgeries. The document dealer responsible for the forgeries was eventually arrested—and not only for the forgeries. He had committed two murders to cover his trail.

If a forged signature can fool experts, it seems unlikely that a signature would not make an effective biometric tool. While a finished signature cannot be used as a biometric tool, the way in which people

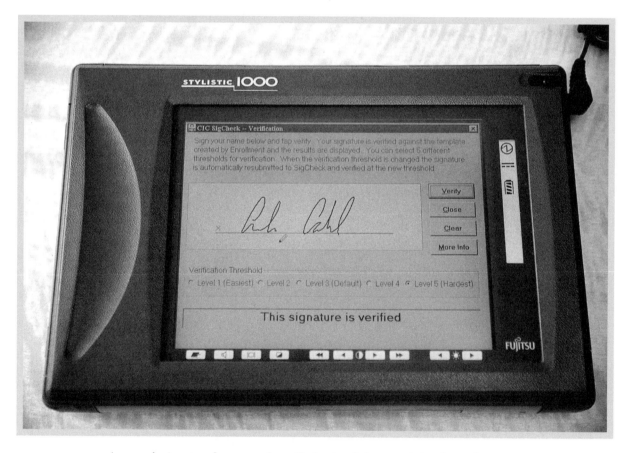

A person's signature has a number of behavioral characteristics that a forger cannot duplicate. Biometric systems that include dynamic signature verification are highly accurate.

sign their name is an effective trait. Each person has a unique way of signing his or her name. Although someone may be able to forge a signature, no one can duplicate the method used to write it. Thus, the process of writing your signature is an excellent behavioral biometric trait.

The process used by a biometric system to verify a signature is called *dynamic signature verification (DSV)*. As a person signs his or her name, a DSV system captures a number of behavioral characteristics with a special sensitive pen and tablet. These characteristics include the angle at which the pen is held, the number of times the pen is lifted, the time taken to write the entire signature, the pressure exerted while holding the pen, and the variations in the speed with which different parts of the signature are written. The sounds a pen makes against the paper as a signature is being written can also be captured. Taken together, these characteristics constitute a behavioral biometric trait.

Each time a person signs his or her name, slight variations can be found in the signature. Thus, several signatures are required from the same person so that an average profile can be compiled. The unique behavioral characteristics are then extracted and coded to form a reference template. This template is used as the basis of comparison any time an individual signs his or her name. The biometric system is typically designed for a "one-to-one" match to verify the individual's identity. Because a forger would not know the dynamics involved in producing a signature, the accuracy of a DSV system is high. DSV is also quite acceptable to most users. They have no problem with the idea of using the way they write their name to establish their identity.

Using Dynamic Signature Verification

Laws enacted in several states provide that a digital signature, such as one used by a DSV system, meets the legal requirements for a valid signature. Thus, digital signatures can be used to sign wills and contracts in

On May 13, 1999, the LCI Technology Group displayed its SMARTpen at a security technology conference in Chicago, Illinois. The SMARTpen is specifically designed for financial and legal transactions requiring a high level of security. The SMARTpen looks and writes like an ordinary ballpoint pen. But that's as far as the similarities go. The SMARTpen is actually a miniature computer. It contains sensors, a mouse, a digital processor, a radio transmitter and receiver, and an encryption system that converts the information into a code.

The sensors inside the SMARTpen capture individual characteristics as a person is signing his or her name. The information is then coded and transmitted by radio frequency to a computer where it is analyzed for a match. The entire process takes about 3 seconds. The SMARTpen utilizes DSV technology. Thus, according to LCI Technology, it is virtually impossible for someone to be falsely accepted by forging a signature. In addition to financial and legal transactions, LCI Technology expects its SMARTpen will find uses in medical, retail, and computer security businesses. According to the company, SMARTpen has two major advantages. It can be used to write on ordinary paper, and it is relatively inexpensive. For just $100 to $250, a customer gets the pen and the software.

California, Florida, Minnesota, Mississippi, Utah, and Washington. On the national level, the U.S. Postal Service recently installed a DSV system to speed up bulk-mail delivery. An individual who wishes to order a bulk mailing signs his or her name on a special pad. If the DSV verifies the signature, the Postal Service can process the order immediately. The Internal Revenue Service (IRS) is testing a biometric signature system that would allow individuals to file their tax returns electronically. The IRS hopes that by 2007, it will receive 80 percent of all tax returns electronically.

DSV is also being used on smart cards. In such cases, the person's signature is replaced with a chip that contains data relating to signature characteristics. To make a purchase or obtain a cash advance, the cardholder signs a special tablet. The signature is electronically compared to the information encoded on the smart card. The transaction is authorized only if a match is made. Because the signature itself is not stored on the card, no one can possibly forge the cardholder's name.

Some financial institutions are hoping to use DSV to eliminate problems associated with printing credit and bank cards without the signature of the user. Currently, many credit cards are stolen before they are delivered to the proper person. If a DSV system were in place, the card manufacturer could be given the signature in an encoded form and the information could be burned into the card with a laser before it is laminated. When the cardholder received his or her card in the mail, the signature would already be there. As a result, it would be more difficult to use stolen credit cards, and people would no longer have to remember to sign the back of a new card before using it.

Keystroke Dynamics

Another behavioral biometric trait is *keystroke dynamics*, commonly known as a typing rhythm. Keystroke dynamics is the unique style that an individual uses when pressing the keys on a keyboard. Thus, a system that uses keystroke dynamics can verify the identity of individuals. This technique was first used by telegraph operators. They learned to identify one another by paying attention to the "fist of the sender"—the speed and rhythm at which the person typed in the code used to transmit the message.

Both the National Science Foundation and the National Institute of Standards and Technology have conducted studies showing that an individual's keystroke dynamics are unique. A biometric system that scans keystroke dynamics monitors the keyboard input thousands of times per second and evaluates the amount of pressure applied to each key, the speed at which the keys are pressed, and the rhythm used. This information is used to make a reference template, which is stored in a central database.

A major advantage of a keystroke dynamic system is that the user may not know that his or her identity is being verified. Thus, the system does not intrude upon the user. In addition, the system is inexpensive because the input device is an existing keyboard. The software needed to enroll users costs less than $50.

Using Keystroke Dynamics

A password is the most widely used method for verifying the identity of a person who seeks access to a computer service or program. Because a password can be stolen, people are reminded not to reveal it indiscriminately and are encouraged to change it periodically.

In an attempt to eliminate the problems associated with passwords, Net Nanny Software International in Bellevue, Washington, has recently released a software program that uses keystroke dynamics to verify an individual's identity. While a user enters his or her password, the software analyzes the person's keystroke dynamics and creates a reference template. Whenever that password is re-entered, the keystroke dynamics are analyzed and compared to the template. The user can access the computer's data only if a match is made. This system makes it nearly impossible for an unauthorized individual to access the computer system, even if he or she has discovered or stolen a valid password.

Unauthorized access to computer systems is a major problem for corporations. More than half of the 1,000 major corporations recently polled said that they had experienced unauthorized use of their computer systems. Some corporations reported that the theft of valuable

Wherever biometric systems that evaluate keystroke dynamics are used, a person who steals an authorized user's password will still be denied access. This system uses dynamic signature verification and keystroke dynamics.

information from their systems represented a loss of more than $1 million. The total loss resulting from unauthorized access to computer systems is estimated to be hundreds of millions of dollars each year.[2] Keystroke dynamics is an inexpensive way for corporations to protect their computer systems from unauthorized use. Keystroke dynamics systems can be used wherever a series of numbers or letters is entered into a keyboard or keypad, such as at ATMs, telephones, and keyless locks.

7 DNA Fingerprinting

IT WAS JUST after midnight on July 17, 1918. Inside a house in a remote village of Russia, eleven people slept soundly. Suddenly, several men burst into the house and told everyone to get out of bed. All eleven people were ordered to dress quickly and then led to the basement of the house.

Among the eleven people were Nicholas II, his wife, and their five children. Just a little more than a year earlier, Nicholas II had been the czar of Russia. His reign had lasted for 23 years. But in 1917, Nicholas II had been forced to give up his throne during a revolution. For the past year, he and his family had been held prisoners in the house.

When Nicholas asked why they were being taken to the basement, he was told that a photograph of the entire group had to be taken immediately. Rumors had spread throughout Russia concerning the whereabouts and safety of the royal family. The photograph would prove that they were still alive and well.

Czar Nicholas II, the last Russian monarch, with his wife, four daughters, and son

Nicholas's wife and son were seated in chairs. The others were told to form two rows behind them. Suddenly, eleven armed men entered the room. One of the guards pulled a piece of paper from his pocket and read it aloud. "In view of the fact that your relatives are continuing their attack on Soviet Russia, the Ural Executive Committee has decided to execute you."[1] Stunned, Nicholas II turned to look at the others. He quickly turned back to the guard and asked "What? What?"[2] After repeating the message, the guard took a revolver from his pocket and shot Nicholas II. The former czar fell to the floor and died instantly.

Before the family could recover from their shock, the armed men began to fire their weapons. Each one had been assigned to kill a specific prisoner and had been told to aim for the heart. In that way, each prisoner would die quickly and without too much bloodshed. But the executions did not go according to plan.

Only five of the prisoners died instantly. The bullet intended for Alexis, Nicholas's son, hit him in the ear. He fell to the floor in agony, and had to be shot a second time. Nicholas's four daughters and the family maid, Demidova, also survived their first shots. The room became chaotic, and the gunmen grew confused. Still, they kept firing. Finally, Alexis and his sisters lay dead on the floor. Demidova, however, was still alive. The executioners eventually silenced her with their bayonets.

With the executions complete, the room was filled with smoke and the smell of gunpowder. Blood had been splattered everywhere. It took a few moments for everything to quiet down. The executioners then took the eleven bodies outside and placed them on a truck. The bodies were driven to an abandoned mine shaft deep in a nearby forest. The executioners lined up the eleven victims on the ground and removed the clothing from each body.

At this point, the executioners realized why the four young girls had not died from their initial gunshot wounds. Each one had hidden part of the family's jewels, mostly diamonds, inside the clothing on their chests.

The diamonds had served as bullet-proof vests for the girls. This explained why the first bullets fired at the girls bounced off, "ricocheting around the room like hail."[3] In all, the executioners collected 18 pounds (8 kg) of diamonds and a large quantity of pearls.

After removing the jewels, the executioners burned the clothing. They struck the bodies with their rifle butts and splashed acid over them. Some historians believe this was done to prevent the bodies from being recognized should they ever be discovered. The bodies were dumped into the mine shaft, which was then sealed shut with soil. Later the bodies were dug up and moved to a new site, but there seemed to be no record of the new grave's location.

Uncovering Nine Skeletons

Historians knew where Nicholas II and his family had been held prisoner, so they were surprised that no one had ever come across their bodies. Then, in 1991, two Russians—one an amateur historian—came across a shallow grave in a swamp. They quickly informed Russian officials, who ordered that the site be dug up. The remains of nine human skeletons were found.

Everyone believed that these skeletons must be the remains of Nicholas II and his family, though they could not explain why two skeletons were missing. The bones were carefully removed from the site and sent to a laboratory for analysis. When scientists examined the skeletons, they realized that none of the bones were young enough to belong to either a 13-year-old or a 17-year-old. Alexis was 13 when he was executed, while his youngest sister, Anastasia, was 17. As a result, some people believed that both Alexis and Anastasia had survived. Others, however, felt that their bodies were buried separately and remained undiscovered. And, in fact, many historians questioned whether any of the bones were actually those of Nicholas II and his family.

To resolve the issue, the bones were sent to England in 1994 for an even more thorough examination. One test revealed that there were five

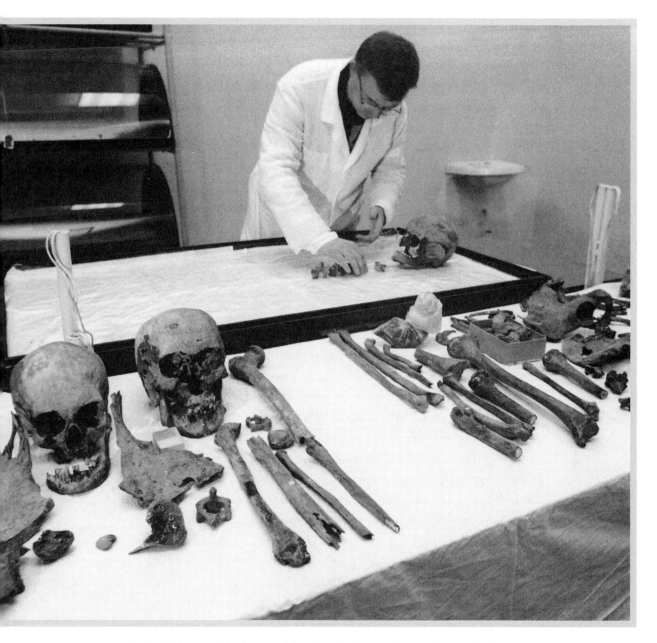

A scientist lays out the bones of the nine skeletons discovered near the house where the czar and his family were murdered.

female and four male bodies in the grave. Another test showed that five of the skeletons belonged to related individuals. Skeletons 4 and 7 were the parents, and skeletons 3, 5, and 6 were their children. Still another test revealed that the children were girls. Along with other evidence that was uncovered, the tests suggested that these skeletons included those of the last Russian czar, his family, and his staff.

On July 17, 1998—exactly 80 years after Nicholas II and his family were executed—the skeletons were buried at a cathedral in St. Petersburg, Russia. The elaborate ceremony lasted 3 days. Dozens of the czar's relatives and diplomats attended the service.

Scientists say there is a 97 percent chance that the skeletons belong to Nicholas II, his wife, three of his children, and four of his household staff. How can scientists make such a claim? They performed a test known as *DNA fingerprinting* on each of the bodies

What Is DNA Fingerprinting?

Everyone—except identical twins—has unique DNA. Thus, DNA is a biometric trait and can be used to establish a person's identity. The order, or sequence, of nucleotide bases in a molecule of DNA forms a kind of code. In 1984, a young British scientist named Alec Jeffreys found a way to read that code.

During reproduction, chromosomes carry all the information contained in our genes from parent to child. When scientists want to talk about all the genes on all our chromosomes, they use the word *genome*. The human genome contains about 100,000 genes and about 3 billion nucleotides. Nearly all the instructions in your genome are identical to the instructions in every other person's genome. Only about 0.01 percent—3 million nucleotides—are different.

Alec Jeffreys was searching for a way to identify a person's 3 million unique nucleotides. He wanted to see exactly what makes each person different from everyone else. Jeffreys knew that a person's 3 million unique rungs are not found all together in one place. They are scattered

Alec Jeffreys in his laboratory

here and there throughout the 3 billion rungs that make up a person's entire genome. They are located in what scientists call *hypervariable regions*—areas of the genome that do not contain genes that carry instructions for assembling amino acids into proteins. In fact, scientists sometimes refer to genes in these regions as "junk DNA" because they have no known function.

When Jeffreys learned about junk DNA, he realized that it might be very useful. Since hypervariable regions are unique in each person, he thought it might be possible to use them to establish identity.

He used a radioactive material to label, or tag, nucleotide bases in the hypervariable regions. When Jeffreys x-rayed his samples, he was amazed by the results. He had hoped to locate a few pieces of DNA located in hypervariable regions. What he saw was a whole complex of banding patterns—alternating gray and black bands stacked on top of one another. Each band represents one of the nucleotide bases that makes up a strand of DNA. Jeffreys called his result a DNA fingerprint. Like the fingerprints on the tips of your fingers, your DNA fingerprints are unique.

Since 1984, Jeffreys process for creating DNA fingerprints has been improved and refined. Today, scientists often couple it with a technique known as the *polymerase chain reaction*, or PCR. This technique can make many copies of a segment of DNA in a very short period of time. As a result, scientists can obtain enough DNA to make a DNA fingerprint from as few as fifty blood cells.

DNA Fingerprints as a Biometric Tool

DNA fingerprinting was used to show that five of the nine skeletons uncovered in Russia in 1991 belonged to related individuals. The banding patterns were so similar that they could come only from people in the same immediate family.

DNA fingerprinting has many practical applications. One of the most important is determining the identity of criminals—even in cases that have gone unsolved for years. In 1996, the New York City Police Department established the Cold Case Squad, a special unit of police detectives who investigate old unsolved cases. Since the unit was formed, the detectives have arrested nearly 600 suspects.

In 1999, detectives arrested a man who was wanted for a murder that had been committed several years earlier. They had uncovered some new evidence. When a DNA analysis was performed on the man's jacket, the banding pattern on the resulting DNA fingerprint matched a DNA fingerprint performed on tissue from the murder victim. Even after several years and even though the jacket had been washed, DNA evidence solved the case.

Unfortunately, investigators are often confronted by suspects who are not legally required to submit to a DNA fingerprint. In such cases, detectives have been known to resort to unusual means to obtain the DNA they need for analysis. In 1999, a man was arrested and charged with three murders based mainly on DNA fingerprints obtained in a rather interesting manner.

While being questioned by the police, the suspect was given a cup of coffee. After he left the police station, investigators grabbed the cup. They were looking for any traces of saliva that the suspect might have left on it. Fortunately, they found enough saliva to provide a DNA sample. The suspect's DNA fingerprint matched those taken from blood samples collected at the scenes of the three murders. Police have arrested other suspects on the basis of DNA fingerprints obtained from cigarette butts or tissues they have casually discarded.

DNA fingerprints can also be used to prove a suspect's innocence. In some cases, DNA fingerprints have made it possible for people in jail to gain their freedom. In the last few years, more than sixty prisoners in the United States have been released from prison due to DNA fingerprint results.

On a cold night in December 1982, the body of a 21-year-old woman was found in her apartment in Oklahoma City, Oklahoma. She

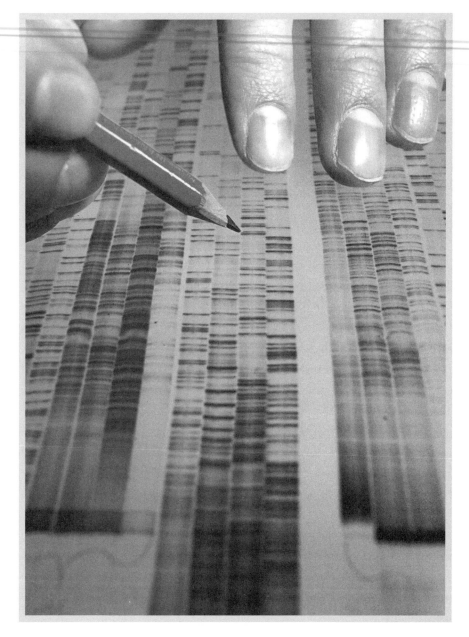

A DNA fingerprint consists of a series of alternating light and dark bands that form a pattern unique to each individual—with the exception of identical twins.

had been raped and then brutally murdered. Five years later, Dennis Fritz and Ronald Williamson were arrested for the murder. Scientific evidence helped convict the two men. Seventeen hairs had been found on the victim's body. An expert from the state crime laboratory testified that some of the hairs were an exact match to those of Fritz, while others matched Williamson's. The expert also testified that semen found on the victim's body could have come from either man.

The jury felt that the evidence proved the men were guilty. Fritz received a life sentence, while Williamson was sentenced to death. According to Mark Barrett, a defense lawyer for Williamson, "This case had all the building blocks of a wrongful conviction."[4] DNA fingerprints from the hairs and semen found on the victim's body did not match those of either Fritz or Williamson. Unfortunately, at the time the men were tried, DNA fingerprints were not admissible as evidence in courts. The technology was too new.

Today, DNA fingerprints can be presented to a jury. When Fritz and Williamson took their case to a court of appeals, their lawyers pointed out that while their clients' DNA fingerprints did not match the ones produced by the hairs or semen, the DNA fingerprint of one of the people who had testified against them did match. In April 1999, Fritz and Williamson were freed after serving 12 years in prison for a murder they didn't commit.

According to Barry Scheck, director of the Innocence Project at the Benjamin Cardozo School of Law in New York and Fritz's lawyer, many prisoners can look forward to freedom because of DNA fingerprinting. In fact, Scheck claims, "We will get thousands out [of jail]."[5] Innocence Project is pushing for the U.S. Congress to pass a law that guarantees any prisoner the chance to have a DNA fingerprint done. Only New York and Illinois currently have such laws.

Just a month after Fritz and Williamson were released from prison, Calvin Johnson was freed from a prison in Georgia where he was serving a life sentence. Again, Innocence Project and a DNA fingerprint were responsible. By the time he was released, however, Johnson had already served 16 years for a crime he did not commit.

In November 1983, an all-white jury in a suburban area just outside Atlanta, Georgia, found Johnson guilty of raping a young white woman. Johnson is an African-American. After hearing the evidence, the jury took only 45 minutes to convict Johnson. The jury was swayed by the testimony of the victim, even though she had failed to pick Johnson out of a police lineup.

They rejected the testimony of four African-American witnesses who all verified Johnson's alibi. The jury also ignored the testimony of an expert from the Georgia State Crime Lab who stated that hairs found on the victim's bedsheets did not match those of Johnson.

A few weeks after he was convicted, Johnson faced another trial—this time in Atlanta—where he was charged with a rape that had similar characteristics. In this case, the jury, which was not all-white, heard the same testimony. The second jury voted for acquittal, but Johnson still faced a life sentence from his first trial.

Through the efforts of Project Innocence, a sample of semen that had been taken from the victim 16 years earlier was turned over for DNA fingerprinting. Johnson's DNA fingerprints did not match any of those found in the semen sample.

Standing on the courthouse steps on the day of Johnson's release, Peter Neufeld of Project Innocence said, "This case hopefully will be a watershed event for the people of Georgia to realize how unreliable eye-witness identification can be."[6]

DNA fingerprints can even be used to exonerate people who may have been mistakenly convicted and executed. In 1986, Joseph O'Dell was convicted of rape and murder in Virginia. He was executed in 1997. During those 11 years, O'Dell's supporters continually raised doubts about his guilt. Now, O'Dell's sister, Sheila Knox, has asked that a DNA fingerprint be performed to prove whether her brother was guilty.

A small amount of semen taken from the murder victim is still locked up in the Virginia Beach County Clerk's Office. (In 1986, PCR technology did not exist, so the sample was not large enough to perform a DNA analysis.) However, Virginia state officials have refused to release the sample. A spokesperson has claimed that if they do, "Every executed inmate in Virginia would want to have his DNA evidence tested after the fact."[7]

The value of DNA fingerprints as a biometric tool extends beyond rape and murder cases. They can be used in paternity cases, and wildlife officials can use them to determine the identity of animal poachers. "We are actually running the equivalent of a homicide investigation," said Kenneth W. Goddard, director of the Fish and Wildlife's Service's National Forensics Laboratory in Ashland, Oregon.[8]

When six headless antelope carcasses were found near a city dump in Casper, Wyoming, investigators canvassed the neighborhood and came up with the name of a suspect. They retrieved the head of an antelope that the suspect had taken to a local taxidermy shop. DNA fingerprints proved that the animal's head belonged to one of the carcasses found at the dump. The suspect was arrested and is now awaiting trial.

DNA fingerprinting technology is still relatively new. In the future, scientists and law-enforcement officials may find even more applications for this technique.

8 Challenges Facing Biometric Systems

IN THE EARLY 1990s, representatives from state welfare agencies, departments of motor vehicles, the Social Security Administration, the Internal Revenue Service, and the Immigration and Naturalization Service formed the Biometric Consortium. The Biometric Consortium has four work groups. The Testing and Reporting Group establishes testing standards. The Database Group collects information into one central database. The Research and Technologies Group keeps abreast of the latest developments in the field of biometrics. The Ground Rules Committee is in charge of public relations and distributes information about the consortium.

In 1995, the group approved a charter that promises to "promote the science and performance of biometrics" for local, state, and federal government agencies. At present, the consortium is studying all biometric systems in use as well as those under development.

In 1997, the consortium established the National Biometric Test Center (NBTC) at San Jose State University in California. Working with both manufacturers and users, the NBTC is developing practical and realistic standards to be used in the testing of biometric systems. Since it was first formed, the NBTC has targeted many of the major problems facing the biometric industry.

When Biometric Devices Don't Work

One of the major problems that the consortium has recognized is referred to as the "missing-body-part" dilemma. According to James Wayman, a researcher at the NBTC, "With any device, some portion of the population—1 to 3 percent—doesn't have that biometric."[1] In other words, some individuals do not have a biometric trait that can be accurately scanned. For example, a mason whose fingers have been damaged from laying bricks for many years might not be an appropriate candidate for a fingerprint scanner. Similarly, a person who has accidentally damaged his or her eye may not be able to use an iris scanner.

Consider the case of Pushp Grover, a native of India who has lived in the United States since 1970. In 1996, she decided to apply for U.S. citizenship. Anyone seeking citizenship is required to provide a set of fingerprints, so that they can be checked against the FBI's files. Grover tried eleven times, but she could not provide a set of fingerprints. Each time her fingers are inked and rolled onto cards, only black smudges appear. She lacks the ridges and whorls that make up normal fingerprints.

Grover is an example of a person who does not have a set of fingerprints that can be used as a biometric trait. Governor Lawton Chiles of Florida is another such person. In 1996, Governor Chiles introduced his state's fingerprint-scanning program for drivers' licenses. When he pressed his thumb on a fingerprint scanner, nothing happened. Then Janet Dennis, a spokeswoman for the Florida Department of Motor

Florida Governor Lawton Chiles is one of the few people who do not have a set of fingerprints that can be used as a biometric trait.

Vehicles tried. In fact, she tried several times. But as Dennis says, "No matter how hard I pressed down, it didn't work."[2] Amazingly, both Chiles and Dennis are among the small percentage of people who cannot be evaluated with that biometric system.

In a study conducted by the Biometric Identification Research Institute in San Jose, California, 2 of the 200 people who had authorized access to a building were repeatedly rejected by a hand scanner.[3] One individual was missing a finger, and the other person had a hand with too may variations to form a usable reference template.

Using a different biometric system, such as a fingerprint scanner, would not solve the company's problem. One employee had an incurable infection that resulted in fingerprints so cracked that they could not be scanned. If either a retinal or an iris scanner were used, individuals with certain eye diseases would not be able to use the system.

This study led people to wonder whether biometric systems are as accurate as reported. Some people claim that the accuracy of such systems has been partly inflated by the way they are tested. For example, one commercial biometric system requires the user to clean his or her fingertip with a water-and-alcohol solution before it is scanned. All the participants in the test followed this regimen, but it is unlikely that all normal users would take this extra step. As dirt and grease build up on the scanner, it would be more likely to give false results.

False Acceptances and False Rejections

Even if this problem can be overcome, the fact remains that no biometric system will ever be 100 percent accurate. As a result, commercial developers often set a *threshold* for their systems. A threshold is the value or score that is designed as part of a biometric system to determine if a match exists. The threshold serves as the reference score that is compared to the actual score obtained whenever a biometric trait is scanned. If the score falls above the threshold, the person is accepted. If the score falls below the threshold, the person is rejected.

The threshold is adjustable. If the threshold is set so that the system has a false acceptance rate of 2 percent, it will incorrectly allow access to 2 of every 100 people who use it. Every biometric system also has a false rejection rate. If the false rejection rate is set at 2 percent, the system will incorrectly refuse to allow access to 2 of every 100 people legitimately enrolled in the database.

A 2 percent false acceptance rate is too high for certain applications. In such circumstances, the biometric system can be designed to have a false acceptance rate close to zero. But this can lead to problems. Reducing the false acceptance rate to lower the probability of falsely accepting an individual results in a system with a high false rejection rate. The reason is simple. To lower the false acceptance rate, manufacturers design a template with more items that must be matched for a positive identification or verification. Thus, the standards for a match are more rigorous.

The more items there are in the template to match, the greater the likelihood that a mistake will be made. Although the system will be less likely to produce a false acceptance, it will also be more likely to produce a false rejection. A biometric system with a false acceptance rate of close to 0 percent will have a false rejection rate of nearly 4 percent. The problem posed by the higher false rejection rate can be overcome to some extent by properly training the individuals who will use the system.

Setting Standards for Certification

At present, no standards have been established for all commercial producers of biometric systems. Nearly 140 biometric-identification products are available, and many more are being developed. In the United States, both the National Biometric Test Center (NBTC) and the International Computer Security Association (ICSA) have developed standards for testing biometric systems. Their goal is to develop a program that will certify systems that meet certain standards.

The NBTC serves as a resource for both the Biometric Consortium and the industry. To achieve its goal of "promoting the use of biometric devices," the NBTC is establishing testing procedures and standards for biometric devices that will include both "human factors requirements and reliability of results."[4] The information obtained will be shared with the government, members of the industry, and users. By sharing such information, the NBTC hopes to "facilitate the cooperation of researchers from many disciplines in the study of biometric identification devices, their uses, and their impact on society."[5]

The ICSA has expressed its desire to "raise the level of public confidence in biometric technology while improving the accuracy and reliability of each product."[6] Only biometric devices with false acceptance and false rejection rates lower than 3 percent are certified by the ICSA. Its certification process involves a 3-month testing period. During this time, each device is subjected to a variety of tests in a two-phase process. The first phase is done in the ICSA laboratory facilities to determine if the device meets minimum standards. If so, the device is then tested by the public in a real-life setting, such as a shopping mall.

The ICSA also guarantees that any biometric and personal data the manufacturer collects from volunteers during the public testing phase will be kept confidential. The association makes this promise because many people are concerned that information provided during the enrollment process might end up in the wrong hands.

Resistance to Biometric Devices

In 1997, the Alabama Department of Motor Vehicles attempted to have a fingerprint scan become part of each driver's license. Motorists were outraged at the idea, and the state withdrew its plans. Since then, a slew of additional studies have shown that Americans distrust biometric systems.

Many people are initially concerned about using a biometric system. Some of their reluctance stems from their lack of knowledge about biometrics. Most people do not know much about biometrics. They do not understand how a biometric system can be used to verify a person's identity. No one can be faulted for being cautious about using something that is unfamiliar.

Even when the operator of a biometric device describes how a system works and explains its benefits, many people remain wary of this new technology. Some people object to fingerprint scanners because they associate fingerprints with criminals. In addition, many people are concerned that biometric systems that use infrared light might endanger their health.

The extent of the public's concern was revealed in a study conducted by Indiana University and released on May 24, 1999.[7] The study found that consumers have very strong feelings about the information they want to reveal and the methods used to obtain such information. The nationwide study involved 2,413 people who tested various biometric systems. The study showed that people dislike information about them being collected and distributed without their knowledge. The respondents also had very negative feelings about the use of biometric devices, as shown in Table 1.

TABLE 1. VIEW OF BIOMETRIC SYSTEMS

System	Like	Dislike
Eye-pattern recognition	8 percent	67 percent
Facial recognition	9 percent	59 percent
Fingerprint scanning	6 percent	57 percent
Voice recognition	10 percent	61 percent

Most people said that they would not approve of a biometric system unless they could understand its benefits. Obviously, the biometric industry has a good deal to do in the way of public education and public relations.

Europeans have a very different attitude about biometrics. In 1999, customers of a British savings and loan institution were asked how they felt about biometric systems. The survey found that 94 percent of the customers had no objection to iris scans. More than 91 percent preferred an iris scan to a PIN or a signature for verification.[8] Because people outside the United States are more accepting of biometric technology, the devices are more widely used in other nations.

The most significant concern expressed by Americans involves preserving personal privacy. Most people are worried that personal information stored in a biometric system's central database might be distributed to other people or other companies. Think about the company that has the faces of 45 million people and information about their buying habits stored in its database. Will they share or sell the data to other companies?

Manufacturers of biometric systems claim that the only purpose of their systems is to identify individuals or to verify an individual's identity. They say that any other use of their systems is totally unacceptable. But who will prevent the systems from being misused? That is a question many people want answered before they support the use of biometric systems.

Measures to Protect Biometric Data

In some cases, the public has already taken measures to prevent biometric systems from becoming operational. There have been several court cases in which individuals have challenged the use of these systems. In each case, the use of the system was upheld by the court. The courts have ruled that the use of biometrics for both identification and verification is perfectly legal.

In March 1999, the International Biometric Industry Association (IBIA) issued a set of "privacy principles" aimed at restricting the distribution of information obtained from retina scans, voice-recognition systems, fingerprint files, and DNA data. According to spokesman Richard

When George was 6 years old, his mother died and his father abandoned him. George's only living relative—an aunt—took him in. Four years later, the aunt was killed in a car accident. From that point on, George was shuffled from one foster home to another. Most did not provide him with a loving and caring environment. Not surprisingly, George started to hang around with the "wrong crowd" when he was 14 years old.

At first, George and his group were only mischievous. They played their music too loud, gathered around the local movie theater late at night, and got suspended from school for fighting. As George and his friends grew older, their antics escalated. When George was 18 years old, he was arrested and convicted of burglary. He was sentenced to 3 years in a jail in Cook County, Illinois. Like all prisoners in the Cook County jail system, George underwent a retinal scan. The scan became part of George's criminal records.

Jail turned out to be a real wake-up call for George. Soon after being locked up, he realized that this was not the type of life he wanted for himself. He became a model prisoner and was released on parole after serving only 16 months of his sentence. George decided to find a good job and start a new life. When George applied for a job as a salesperson, the company requested his medical records. That's when George's troubles really began.

As it turns out, a retinal scan can do more than verify a person's identity. It can also provide information about a person's

Norton, "The IBIA believes the private sector should set forth clear policies on how biometric data will be stored and used and collected, and that individuals have the right to know when data is being collected, and they should have the right to limit distribution of that

health. The retinal scan taken by the Cook County Sheriff's Office revealed that George had high blood pressure. The company refused to give George a job because it was concerned that George's high blood pressure might cause him to "blow his top" if he confronted an irritating customer.

After much searching, George was finally able to find a job. The salary was not great, but it was enough to pay his bills. Unfortunately, the job did not provide medical insurance. Putting aside a little from each paycheck, George was eventually able to seek medical coverage on his own. Once again, the insurance company asked for his medical records.

When they analyzed the retinal scan, the results revealed that George had diabetes. Even though the condition could be managed through diet, the insurance company refused to enroll him. No matter how hard George tried, he could not get any company to provide medical coverage.

This is not a true story, but it could be. Abrasions on the retina show up on a retinal scan. Certain abrasions can be a sign that a person has high blood pressure, diabetes, or even AIDS. To protect an individual's privacy, consumer-advocate groups insist that a biometric scan should be used solely for identification purposes. Any other information should not become part of the individual's record, and it certainly should not be shared or sold. What do you think?

---

data."[10] So far, the IBIA has not come up with a set of specific recommendations because there are too many possible scenarios.

According to Simon Davies, founder of the watch group Privacy International, "The point is that once biometric data has been collected and used on a public system, it is impossible to stop it completely from spreading, being used for other purposes."[11] Davies claims that the very fact that there are so many different scenarios is the problem.

Some states have passed laws to prevent commercial enterprises from obtaining biometric data gathered by others. California's state legislature is currently considering at least a dozen bills that deal with biometric privacy.

One bill would prevent the use of biometric information for any purpose other than that for which it was designed and would prohibit people, businesses, and institutions from:

■ selling or sharing biometric identifier data with other people, businesses, or institutions, except law-enforcement agencies, the State Department of Social Services, and county welfare departments.

■ collecting information about an individual without notice and consent.

■ collecting or using information to discriminate on any unlawful basis.[9]

To prevent problems related to privacy issues from arising, California is considering another bill that would impose a $10,000 fine on any insurance company, health maintenance organization (HMO), or pharmaceutical supplier that knowingly sells or shares medical information, including biometric data. In addition, the IBIA has suggested that both commercial and government biometric systems develop the technology needed to protect the confidentiality of their databases.

The Client Identification and Benefits System Department in Ontario, Canada, is currently testing a fingerprint-scan system that makes it easier for people eligible for social assistance to receive their benefits quickly. This system guarantees the privacy of users. Templates of the fingerprint scans can only be accessed with a court order. In addition, a template alone cannot be used to identify an individual.

Some people suggest that the concerns about invasion of privacy can be avoided by designing biometric systems without databases. These people recommend a "one-to-one" matching system. With a "one-to-one" system, the biometric information is on a smart card, not in a database. Whenever an individual uses a biometric scanner, he or she also inserts the smart card into the system. The system simply compares the scan with the biometric data on the smart card.

Educating the Public

Many biometrics companies feel that concerns about their products can best be addressed by educating the public. People must understand that a biometric system has just two uses—to identify and recognize an individual or to verify his or her identity. These systems have not been designed for any other purpose. People who hesitate to use the technology must be made comfortable with biometric systems. When ATMs made their first appearance some 20 years ago, many people were wary of them. Today, it's hard to imagine life without them. Perhaps, one day, people will feel the same way about biometric systems.

9 The Future of Biometrics

BIOMETRICS IS A burgeoning business. In 1998, more than $500 million was spent worldwide on biometric devices. More of this money was spent on fingerprint-scanning devices than on any other kind of biometric system. In 2001, sales of fingerprint-scanning systems alone are expected to reach $1 billion.[1] This money will be spent by a variety of government agencies and private corporations to monitor immigration and employee work schedules, to eliminate fraud in licensing and entitlement programs, and to limit access to certain facilities and sites.

As biometric technology continues to advance, the cost of systems will decrease. In 1994, the smallest fingerprint scanner was the size of a telephone and cost $2,000. In 1999, a scanner that could do the same job was the size of two sugar cubes and cost just $99. In 2003, the same device will probably sell for about $15.[2]

At the same time, biometric systems will become increasingly sophisticated and accurate. For example, Visionics

Corporation in Jersey City, New Jersey, has recently developed a facial-scanning system that can identify a moving face in a crowd. The system uses fifty characteristics to create an eigenface that is compared to a database containing thousands—or even millions—of pictures. Several major airports have expressed interest in this kind of system.

In 1998, the Ultra-Scan Company in Buffalo, New York, unveiled a two-finger scanner. Although two-finger scanners had been available for some time, they required the user to place his or her fingers on the scanner in the same order as when the data was first captured. This was a problem because many users forgot the order in which they originally placed their fingers on the scanner.

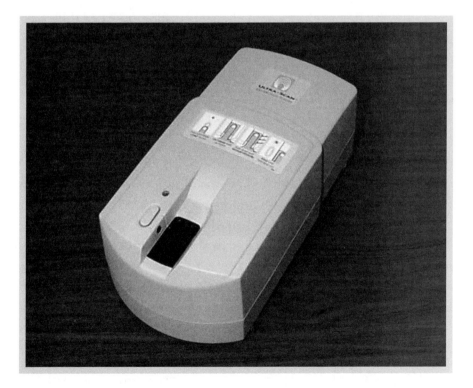

Newly developed two-finger scanners are more accurate and easier to use than older models.

Ultra-Scan's system allows users to place either finger on the scanner first. The Ultra-Scan system creates an image with ultrasound waves, which results in a very high-quality image. This makes the system particularly useful for clients who want small children to use the system.*

In 1998, Ultra-Scan conducted a test of its new two-finger scanner in a federal prison in Argentina. The system captured 12,000 images from 3,000 inmates, employees, and visitors to verify their identity. According to Ultra-Scan, "The test did not record a single failure."[3]

New Applications for Biometric Devices

In April 1999, Robert Bulaga and Michael Moshier unveiled their new invention. They designed the Solo Trek Exo-Skeletor Flying Vehicle to commute to work. According to Bulaga, "The traffic here [Santa Clara, California,] is horrible. I'd love to be able to fly to work in this."[4]

It took the inventors 3 years and $1 million to develop the 8-foot (2.4-m)-tall machine that looks like a giant bug. The pilot climbs inside the vehicle, straps in, and uses handles to control the machine's tilt and speed. The flying machine travels up to 80 miles (128 km) per hour, climbs to 10,000 feet (3,050 m), and runs on regular gasoline. It can land anywhere a person can stand. Moshier predicts that the flying machine will cost about the same as a luxury car when it reaches the commercial market.

Bulaga and Moshier are concerned that people might try to fly the machine without the proper training. "The last thing we want is John Q.

---

* Children 5 years of age and younger present a challenge to fingerprint-scanning devices because the ridges that make up their fingerprints are very fine and very close together. Most finger scanners are not capable of capturing the details of a young child's fingerprint.

A retinal scanner restricts use of this rather strange looking flying machine to those who have completed the training program.

Public to get in one of these things and go out and kill themselves," they said.[5] To prevent this from happening, the inventors installed a retinal-scanning system in the cockpit. The machine cannot be operated unless the pilot's retinal scan matches one from a database of people who have passed the training program.

DNA Fingerprinting

One biometric system that has undergone major technological advances is DNA fingerprinting. At one time, it took 16 weeks to get results. Now it takes just 3 days. In addition, the cost for preparing a single DNA fingerprint has dropped from $5,000 to about $80.

DNA fingerprints are extremely useful to law-enforcement officials. They have been used to establish the guilt of dangerous felons, even when the crimes were committed many years ago. This same technology has found limited use outside courtrooms, however. DNA fingerprints cannot be used in biometric scanning systems because it takes too long to get results. In addition, DNA fingerprinting cannot be considered user-friendly. In most cases, an individual must submit a sample of blood or some other body tissue. To broaden the appeal of DNA fingerprinting for use in biometric systems, researchers are looking for ways to speed up the process and make it user-friendly.

New Biometric Traits

Scientists are also searching for new physical and behavioral traits that can be used in biometric systems. For example, researchers are evaluating a system that uses an infrared camera to capture the pattern of veins on the back of a person's hand. Areas of the hand with no veins reflect infrared light. This reflected light passes through a special filter on the camera, producing a light and indistinct image on the film. A darker and sharper image is obtained for the vein pattern because the blood vessels absorb infrared light. Thus, the image captured by the camera represents the unique pattern formed by the veins on the back of a person's hand. So far, researchers have determined that the system records the best images when the user's fist is clenched so that the skin on the hand is taut.

In May 1999, Neusciences Limited, a company located in Southampton, England, announced that it had developed the first commercial biometric system based on vein patterns in the hand. They call their new system Veincheck. It consists of a computer fitted with a video camera. Special filters are used to enhance the images of the veins. When someone wishes to enter an area secured by Veincheck, he or she presents a smart card that contains an encoded copy of his or her vein pattern. The individual then inserts one hand into a scanner, which creates an image of the vein pattern. If the image matches the pattern on the smart card, the person is allowed access to the facility.

Other researchers are evaluating a very different biometric trait—body odor. They are developing sensors that absorb the chemicals responsible for the odor an individual emits. Such odors play a very important role in communication among animals. But humans look upon body odor as socially unacceptable and aesthetically unappealing. Deodorants are used to prevent it, and lotions and perfumes are applied to mask it.

These products do not stop the body from emitting chemicals through the skin, so they can be used as a biometric trait. When a sensor picks up the chemicals an individual secretes through his or her skin, that information can be converted into an electronic code and used to form a reference template.

Public acceptance of a biometric system that analyzes a person's body odor remains highly questionable. Other biometric traits that would be more acceptable and that are currently being tested include ear and lip shape, knuckle creases, and the heat emitted by a person's organs.

The Long-Term Costs of Biometric Systems

Because biometrics is a relatively new technology, most of the agencies and businesses using biometric devices have yet to reap the benefits claimed by manufacturers. One such benefit is saving money.

In June 1998, Arizona installed a fingerprint-scanning system to verify the identity of people who receive state benefits. Since that time, an average of fifty-seven individuals have been removed from the state's benefit rolls each month. These people were cheating the system by collecting money they were not eligible for. By the end of 2002, state officials predict that a total of 2,850 people will have been removed from the system.

By that time, Arizona will have spent more than $4 million dollars on its fingerprint-scanning program. At first glance, this may seem like a lot of money, but if those people had continued to collect benefits, it would have cost the state more than $10 million. Thus, Arizona state officials expect the fingerprint-scanning system will save the state $6 million of taxpayers' money.[6]

Biometric systems have already saved the state of New York money. The New York State Department of Social Services requires a fingerprint scan for all residents who receive benefits. The main goal of the scanning system is to identify people who are using false names to receive additional benefits. In the first 19 months of the program, nearly 1 million people were enrolled in the fingerprint-scanning system. During that time, 172 cases of fraud were detected. The program also saved money by discouraging additional people from trying to beat the system. Since the finger scanners were introduced, New York has removed nearly 37,000 names from its entitlement rolls. This saved the state $314 million.[7]

State agencies are not the only ones who have, or will, save money by using biometric systems. Many companies have installed biometric systems to eliminate the practice of "buddy punching" in which one employee signs in for another. Banks will benefit because fewer people will be able to cash bad checks or misuse ATM machines.

In 1998, Kroger grocery stores decided to combat the problem of check fraud. Kroger wanted to be sure that the checks their stores cashed were valid, but they did not want to inconvenience their customers. Because an average of 15,000 people shop at a Kroger store each day, company executives realized they would have to choose a system that involved a minimal amount of training.

Store customers had made it clear that they did not want to have PIN numbers, so Kroger decided to install a two-finger scanning system. It takes about 30 seconds for a customer to enroll in the system. The system scans one finger from each hand, does an internal quality check, and then enrolls the individual in the program.

From that point on, the customer simply submits to a finger scan at checkout time. This scan takes only 2 seconds to process. If a match is made, the individual can use a check. The customer can also cash a check, including his or her paycheck. The system is so fast and easy to use that Kroger calls it "the touch and go system."[8]

Kroger discovered that some customers were initially concerned about the issue of privacy. When the store guaranteed customers that no personal information would be passed to the management or the store's employees, most customers seemed satisfied.

Invasion of Privacy

The future of biometric systems depends in large measure on how their manufacturers handle the issue of invasion of privacy. Critics argue that biometric systems will make it easy for anyone to obtain personal information about people enrolled in the system. Some have even gone so far as to propose that any information obtained by a biometric system not be entered into a central database.

In April 1999, Representative Ron Paul of Texas voiced his opinion. "It seems like everywhere you turn there's another . . . attempt to accumulate more information about us," Paul said.[9] He wants to prevent government agencies from assembling massive databases of DNA fingerprints, retinal scans, and facial scans. Representative Paul's concern about invasion of privacy stems from a recent revelation that Image Data, a company located in Nashua, New Hampshire, purchased 22 million drivers' license photographs to start a national database of images.

The company obtained the photographs from three states—Florida, Colorado, and South Carolina. Part of the money the company used to purchase the photographs came from U.S. government funds, specifically from the Secret Service. When the story appeared in newspapers and on television, many people were outraged. Florida and Colorado immediately halted further sales of their photographs, and South Carolina sued to get theirs back.

Big Brother Is Watching You

In 1949, George Orwell wrote a novel called *1984*. In the story, Big Brother and The Party control every aspect of the lives of the citizens who live in Oceania. The Party consists of two groups. Those in The Inner Party make all the laws and its members live in luxury, while those in The Outer Party do all the work. More than 80 percent of The Outer Party consists of "proles" who are considered intellectually inferior by the others.

All the workers, especially the proles, must contribute to Big Brother's plan to conquer its rivals in Eastasia and Eurasia. Big Brother does not actually exist. Rather, Big Brother is a creation of The Inner Party to control the workers of The Outer Party. Signs posted everywhere claim that "Big Brother Is Watching You."

Stories about other misuses of personal information also appeared. The *Christian Science Monitor* reported that Infoglide, a technology company in Austin, Texas, was able to piece together information to find out that people who drive old Volvo cars are more likely to eat fat-free yogurt than most other people are.[10] Critics of biometric systems point out that such information could be exploited by yogurt companies. These critics equate the growing use of biometric systems with George Orwell's "Big Brother."

Supporters of Biometrics

Supporters claim that comparing biometric systems to a "Big Brother" scenario is unjustified. They do not believe that biometric systems will violate personal privacy. In fact, they say, these systems will actually accomplish just the opposite. They protect the privacy of users.

One worker, Winston Smith, is a secret enemy of The Party. He hopes that someday the proles will rebel and overthrow The Party. Winston falls in love with Julia, another Outer Party member. Together, they plot with O'Brien, a member of The Inner Party, to overthrow The Party. O'Brien claims to harbor a hatred for The Inner Party, but he turns out to be one of its most powerful members.

O'Brien reveals the plan devised by Winston and Julia. The two are taken to the Ministry of Love where they are programmed by The Party to love and respect Big Brother. The two no longer have any thoughts other than those programmed by The Party. Winston is eventually taken back to the Ministry of Love and is shot.

First, supporters point out that the use of biometric systems is entirely legal. For example, biometric systems do not violate the U.S. Constitution, specifically the Fourth and Fifth Amendments.

The Fourth Amendment protects citizens from unreasonable search and seizure. Supporters claim that scanners used in biometric systems do not perform such searches. The Fourth Amendment also guarantees "The right of people to be secure in their persons, houses, papers, and effects." Supporters claim that regulations and guidelines can prevent the distribution of personal information that is obtained about an individual by a biometric system. As an example, supporters point to the four privacy principles issued by the International Biometric Industry Association (IBIA).

1. Biometric data are formatted in electronic code that is separate and distinct from personal information, and provides an effective, secure barrier against unauthorized access to personal information. Beyond this inherent protection, IBIA recommends safeguards to ensure that biometric data are not misused to compromise any information, or released without personal consent or the authority of law.

2. In the private sector, IBIA advocates the development of policies that clearly set forth how biometric data will be collected, stored, accessed, and used, and that preserve the rights of individuals to limit the distribution of the data beyond the stated purposes.

3. In the public sector, IBIA believes that clear legal standards should be developed to carefully define and limit the conditions under which agencies of national security and law enforcement may acquire, access, store, and use biometric data.

4. In both the public and private sectors, IBIA advocates the adoption of appropriate managerial and technical controls to protect the confidentiality and integrity of databases containing biometric data.

The Fifth Amendment protects citizens against self-incrimination. Supporters of biometrics point out that submitting to a biometric scan is no more self-incriminating than providing law-enforcement officials with a set of traditional fingerprints.

The Value of Biometrics

Even though the issue of privacy continues to be debated, most people cannot deny that biometric systems are a powerful tool for identification and verification. Perhaps their value can best be appreciated by looking at a simple science project conducted by an eighth grader named Shanin Leeming.

Shanin, a student at Divine Mercy Catholic School on Merritt Island, Florida, decided to test whether a photo ID is a valid way to verify a person's identity. She conducted a series of ten tests to see if people would challenge someone who looked different from the photograph on the ID they presented. Shanin enlisted the help of her mother.

Shanin started by making simple changes to her mother's facial appearance. For the first trial, she stuffed her mother's cheeks with cotton to change the shape of her face. Her mother passed through airport security without a problem. Her mother's second disguise included a baseball cap, a wig, a fake mustache, dark glasses, and a tatoo. Shanin's mother was able to cash a check in this disguise.

Her other disguises included a clown suit complete with face paint, a vampire's costume, and a man's outfit including dreadlock hair, a mustache, and an 8-inch (20-cm) tattoo. Shanin used mortician's wax on her mother's face to give the "man" an older, mask-like appearance. While in line at the checkout, Shanin even called the "man" "Grandpa."

Only once was Shanin's mother challenged. But when her mother produced a second photo ID, her check was cashed! Shanin's simple science project clearly points out the need for a better system of identifying people. Biometrics is certainly one possibility.

This is what Shanin Leeming's mother looked like in her second disguise. Would you let this "character" cash a check with an ID that shows a normal-looking woman?

Glossary

amino acid—a building block of proteins

biometric trait—a unique, measurable physical or behavioral feature that can be used to recognize or verify a person's identity

biometrics—the study and analysis of biometric traits

capillary—a tiny blood vessel that connects an artery to a vein

chromosome—a rod-shaped structure in the nucleus made up of DNA and protein

DNA (deoxyribonucleic acid)—a chemical compound that serves as the hereditary material of a cell

DNA fingerprinting—the process of treating DNA so that a pattern of bands is produced for analysis

double helix—a common name for DNA, referring to the double-stranded, spiraling structure of the molecule

dynamic signature verification (DSV)—a biometric system used to verify an individual's signature

eigenface—a two-dimensional arrangement of light and dark areas that represents an image of a face

embryo—a human being or other living thing in the earliest stages of development

facial thermogram—an image formed by the heat released from small blood vessels just beneath the skin on the face

false acceptance—the incorrect verification of an impostor

false rejection—the failure to correctly identify an individual as being a legitimate member of a data bank

gamete—a sperm or egg cell

gene—the basic unit of hereditary

genetic recombination—the process by which homologous chromosomes exchange portions with one another

genome—all the genes in a human body

heredity—the transfer of traits from parent to child through genes

hypervariable regions—the areas of the human genome that do not carry genetic instructions, also called "junk DNA"

iris—the pigmented layer of the eye that controls the size of the pupil

keystroke dynamics—the unique style an individual uses when pressing the keys on a keyboard

larynx—commonly known as the voice box because it contains the vocal cords that produce sounds

meiosis—the process of cell division that readies a sperm or egg for fertilization *minutiae*–the marks left on a surface by the points where two ridges on a fingertip meet

mitosis–the process of cell division that produces two cells that are genetically identical to the original cell

nucleotide–a unit, or building block, of a gene

nucleus–the part of the cell that controls most of its activities

polymerase chain reaction–a cloning process used to make a large number of copies of a DNA sequence from very little DNA material for the purpose of DNA fingerprinting

reference template–a mathematical code that represents a biometric trait of an individual

retina–the light-sensitive inner layer of the eye

smart card–a wallet-sized card that contains a microchip encoded with certain information

speech-recognition system–a system that uses a voice pattern to identify an individual

threshold–a value or score that is designed as part of a biometric system to determine if a match exists

voice print–a template of a voice pattern that is used to establish the identity of an individual

voice verification–a system that uses a voice pattern to establish an individual's identity

Endnotes

Chapter 1

1. Ross, Bobby and John Perry. "Witnesses Describe Reactions When Blast Occurred." *The Oklahoman Online Archives*. April 20, 1995. Internet page at URL: <archives.oklahoman.com/cgi-bin/fget?filename=/archive/bombing/>.
2. *The Oklahoman Online Archives*, ibid.
3. *The Oklahoman Online Archives*, ibid.

Chapter 3

1. "Handing it to Biometrics." *Security Management*. February 1998, p. 14.
2. Prucell, F. J. Bud. "Biometrics for the Uninitiated." *Manage*. February 1998, p. 16.
3. Zamora, Jim Herron. "Daly City Man Held in Heist on Credit Card Info." *San Francisco Examiner*. May 22, 1997. Internet page at URL: <http://www.sfgate.com/cgibin/article.cgi?file=/examiner/archive/1997/05/22/NEWS712.dtl>.
4. SAC Technologies. Internet page at URL: <http://www.sacman.com/biometrics_explained/tutorials/pagea04.htm>.

5. SAC Technologies. Internet page at URL: <http://www.sacman.com/biometrics_explained/biobig.html>.

6. SAC Technologies. Internet page at URL: <http://www.sacman.com/current_news/1999/may1399.html>.

Chapter 4

1. AIMS Education Foundation, 1998. Internet page at URL: <http://www.aimsedu.org/activities/gimmefive/gimme2.html>.

2. Identix Corporate Information. Internet page at URL: <http://www.identix.com/corporate/news/1999/transcript.html>.

3. The Children's Safety Center at URL: http://www.kidsbesafe.com.

Chapter 5

1. *Biometrics in Human Resources*, June 1999. Internet page at URL: <http://www.dss.state.ct.us/digital/news14/bhsug14.html>.

2. *Automatic ID News*. Internet page at URL: <http://www.autoidnews.com/technologies/concepts/retinal.htm>.

3. Spring Technologies, Inc. Internet page at URL: <http://www.springtechnic.com/irisrec.html>.

4. Wheeler, Michael D. "Facial Recognition System Verifies Driver's Identity." *Technology News*. June 1998. Internet page at URL: <http://www.laurin.com/Content/Jun98/techFacial.html>.

5. Wheeler, ibid.

Chapter 6

1. CAVE: The Case for Speaker Verification. Internet page at URL: <http://www.ptt-telecom.nl/cave/apologia.html>.

2. Computer & Internet Security Resources. Internet page at URL: <http://virtuallibrarian.com/legal/ccstatistics.html>.

Chapter 7

1. Massie, Robert K. *The Romanovs: The Final Chapter*. New York: Random House, 1995, p. 5
2. Massie, ibid.
3. Massie, ibid.
4. Dedman, Bill. "DNA Tests Are Freeing Scores of Prison Inmates." *New York Times*. April 19, 1999, p.12
5. Dedman, ibid.
6. Firestone, David. "DNA Test Brings Freedom, 16 Years After Conviction." *New York Times*. June 16, 1999, p. 22.
7. Cohen, Adam. "A Sister's Plea: Test the DNA." *Time*. June 28, 1999, p. 8.
8. Sink, Mindy. "Genetic Pawprints Are Leading Game Wardens to the Poachers." *New York Times*, May 26, 1998, p. 22.

Chapter 8

1. Davis, Ann. "The Body as Password." *Wired Magazine*. Internet page at URL: <http://www.wired.com/wired/5.07/biometrics.html>.
2. WinonaNet. July 13, 1997. Internet page at URL: <http://www.winonanet.com/extras/1997/life/L07139701.html>.
3. WinonaNet, ibid.
4. National Biometric Test Center Internet page at URL: <http://www-engr.sjsu.edu/~graduate/biometrics/.
5. National Biometric Test Center, ibid.
6. ICSA Internet page at URL: <http://www.icsa.net/services/consortia/>.
7. Summary of Indiana University report available at Internet page at URL: <http://www.dss.state.ct.us/pubs/BIOMET_BREAKING_%20NEWS.html>.

8. Gugliotta, Guy. "Bar Codes to the Body Make It to the Market." *Washington Post.* June 21, 1999. p. A1.

9. Laws and Legislation. Internet page at URL: http://www.iosoftware.com/about/laws.htm>.

10. Kriz, Heid. "Boosting Biometric Privacy." *Wired News.* March 30, 1999. Internet page at URL: <http://www.wired.com/news/news/technology/story/18810.html>.

11. Kriz, ibid.

Chapter 9

1. Surtees, Lawrence. "Your Secret Identity." *Globetechnology.com.* December 10, 1998. Internet page at URL: <http://www.globetechnology.com/gam/News/19981210/TWBIOM.html>.

2. Sherrid, Pamela. "You Can't Forget This Password." *Business and Technology.* May 17, 1999, p. 17. Internet page at URL: <http://www.usnews.com/usnews/issue/990517/17biom.htm>.

3. Ultra-Scan Company Report. December, 1998. Internet page at URL: <http://www.ultrascan.com/new.htm>.

4. "Inventors Take Page from Jetsons." *The Salt Lake City Tribune.* April 27, 1999. Internet page at URL: <http://www.sltrib.com/1999/apr/04271999/nation_w/101096.htm>.

5. *The Salt Lake City Tribune*, ibid.

6. Biometrics in Human Services. March 1999. Internet page at URL: <http://dss.state.ct.us/digital/news13/bhsug13.html>.

7. Hearing of the Subcommittee on Domestic and International Monetary Policy, U.S. House of Representatives. May 20, 1998. Internet page at URL: <http://commdocs.house.gov/committee/bank/hba48784.000/hba48784_0.htm>.

8. Hearing of the Subcommittee on Domestic and International Monetary Policy, U.S. House of Representatives, ibid.

9. McCullagh, Declan. "DNA Databases Go Too Far." *Wired News.* April 26, 1999. Internet page at URL: <http://www.wired.com/news/news/politics/story/19338.html>.

10. Belsie, Laurent. "Slide Toward Surveillance Society." *Christian Science Monitor*. February 26, 1999. p. 1. Internet page at URL: <http://www.csmonitor.com/durable/1999/02/26/fp1sl-csm.shml>.

To Find Out More

Books

Coleman, Howard and Eric Swenson. *DNA in the Courtroom: A Trial Watcher's Guide*. Genelex: Seattle, WA, 1994.

Jones, Charlotte F. *Fingerprints & Talking Bones: How Real-Life Crimes Are Solved*. Delacorte: New York, 1997.

Lampton, Christopher. *DNA Fingerprinting*. Franklin Watts: Danbury, CT, 1991.

Organizations and Online Sites

THE BIOMETRIC CONSORTIUM
  http://www.biometrics.org/

  The Biometric Consortium serves as the U.S. government's focal point for research, development, and testing of biometric systems. This site has links to an introduction about biometrics, examples of biometric systems, and information about standards.

COMPUTERWORLD

http://www.computerworld.com/

Enter the keyword "biometrics" in your search for information. Be sure to specify the time period in month, day, and year that you would like to search.

EDN MAGAZINE

http://www.ednrnag.corm /1998/050798/10cs.cfm

This site has an article that summarizes various aspects of biometrics. Numerous links are provided, including ones that lead to manufacturers of biometric products. You can also reach the senior technical editor through the phone numbers listed or via the e-mail address that is linked to this site.

INTERNATIONAL BIOMETRIC GROUP

http://www.biometricgroup.com

The International Biometric Group is a private firm that provides biometric consulting services, including biometric research data, classes, and seminars. A section of its home page is titled "Biometrics in the News."

INTERNATIONAL BIOMETRIC INDUSTRY ASSOCIATION

http://www.ibia.org/

The International Biometric Industry Association (IBIA) was founded in 1998 to advance the interests of the biometric industry. Links include general information about biometrics and a search tool.

The International Computer Security Association
http://www.icsa.net/

This site has a link called Tech Zone that leads to information on biometrics. You can also download the biometric survey.

Introduction to Biometrics
http://www.choiceadvantage.com/Biometrics/Biometrics.htm

This site contains a comprehensive article dealing with the general history of biometrics and a summary of biometric systems. The basic operation of each system is described, along with a table grading its accuracy, ease of use, barrier to attack, public acceptability, and long-term stability.

Wired News
http://www.wired.com/news/news/search_results_news?words= biometrics

This site provides an updated summary of articles dealing with bio-metrics.

INDEX

ABOUT THE AUTHOR

SALVATORE TOCCI taught chemistry and biology at East Hampton High School on Long Island, New York, for many years. Because he believes that science is learned best when students are actively involved in the process, he has written many science project books for high school students. He has also written several books about diseases and a high school textbook that focuses on the practical applications of chemistry. While Mr. Tocci was a teacher, he organized many science fairs at his school. He continues to judge local, regional, and national contests. Mr. Tocci has also presented workshops for science teachers at meetings held throughout the United States.